£4.00

BRITAIN'S RAIL SUPER CENTRES

LONDON
– THE GREAT WESTERN LINES

BRITAIN'S RAIL SUPER CENTRES

LONDON

– THE GREAT WESTERN LINES

IAN ALLAN Publishing

LAURENCE WATERS

First published 1993

ISBN 0 7110 2164 3

Published by Ian Allan Ltd, Shepperton, Surrey; and printed by Ian Allan Printing Ltd at their works at Coombelands in Runnymede, England.

Contents

Preface

When asked by Ian Allan to produce a 'Britain's Rail Super Centres' book on the Great Western lines out of Paddington I had to make a decision as to just what to cover. As I had written *Rail Centres: Reading* a few years ago it seemed logical to link up with the Reading book and cover the Great Western line eastwards from Twyford. This has also enabled me to cover all of the Great Western branch lines that have emanated (or still do) from what are today termed the 'Thames' and 'Chiltern' lines.

Information on the history and working of the lines has been found in the following locations: Public Record Office, Kew, the Bodleian Library, and the Great Western Trust Collection, Didcot Railway Centre.

Other sources have been: *The Great Western Magazine, Trains Illustrated, Railway World, Railway Magazine, Locomotive Review, Bradshaws Guides, Railway Observer, Journal of Transport History* and many BR timetables and working instructions.

Sources and Acknowledgements

I would like to thank the following individuals and associations for supplying photographs and other material for this book: A. A. Delicata, R. C. Riley, Stanley Creer, Brian Morrison, Paul Karau, John Edwards, Hugh Ballantyne, Leslie Sandler, Dr Geoff Smith, Paul Shannon, David Collins, Derek Tuck, Phil Kelley, David Sellman, C. R. L. Coles, Kevin Lane, Eddie Lyons, the Ian Allan Library, the Great Western Trust, the Industrial Railway Society and the Signalling Record Society.

Special thanks to Tony Walker (Station Manager Paddington) Andrew Chivers (Depot Manager Old Oak Common), Hans Mueller of Plasser Railway Machinery (GB) Ltd, and staff of the Kegging and Archive departments at Guinness Park Royal.

Also special thanks are due to Peter Webber and Dr Rosemary Painter for the laborious task of checking the manuscript.

Laurence Waters   Oxford
March 1993

Frontispiece:
The rather interesting letterbox at the now demolished Paddington Goods. *Great Western Trust*

Previous page:
The up 'Capitals United Express', the 8am service from Cardiff, approaches arrival Platform No 9 in January 1959 hauled by 'Britannia' Pacific No 70029 *Shooting Star*. *Spencer Yeats*

1. Introduction

Of all the lines running into London it is the Great Western main line into Paddington that always seems to conjure up the most interest and romanticism. Why is this? I suppose one could answer it with one word: Brunel.

Brunel was probably the greatest engineer that this country has known. Today his statue surveys the Lawn at Paddington and his remains are buried adjacent to the railway line at Kensal Green Cemetery. The Great Western was Brunel's railway and it is a mark of his genius that some 145 years after his death High Speed Trains are travelling along what is essentially the same trackbed, albeit on a different gauge, to and from his crowning glory — Paddington.

'Hall' class 4-6-0 No 5922 *Caxton Hall* climbs the bank from Acton with a Cheltenham Spa-Wembley schoolboys' International special on 27 April 1963.
C. T. Robinson

2. London

Some 3,000 years ago the site of London comprised only a few farming communities and it was not until the arrival of the Romans in 43AD that Londinium was established. It was at this point on the Thames that Plautus constructed a bridge during his march from Richborough (Kent) to set up his capital at Camulodunum (Colchester)

The Romans found that the Thames provided a good method of transporting supplies into the country, and a small settlement soon grew up around the northern side of the bridge. Gradually the settlement grew into a large town but, in 60AD, it was attacked and destroyed by Boudicca. It was subse-

quently rebuilt by the Romans and, by the end of the first century AD, had superseded Colchester as the most important centre in the land and, with the construction of many roads, became the hub of communications. Even after the Romans left in 410AD the importance of the port and road system continued to ensure that London remained the most important city in the land.

Since those early days the population of London has continued to grow but it was not until the 19th and 20th centuries that the city expanded outwards to any great degree.

Some idea of the rapid increase in the population during the last 200 years can be gleaned from the fact that by 1700 the population of London had risen to about 600,000; in 1801 it had doubled to some 1,110,000 but in the ensuing years up to 1890 there was a staggering six fold increase to 6,580,000. Some of this growth can be directly attributed to the improvement in road, rail and river transport which in turn brought more jobs; this greater prosperity allowed the population to spread outwards into the suburbs.

Prior to the coming of the railways those wishing to travel to and from London had the choice of using either river, canal, foot or horse for transport. Those who could afford it were able to live outside the city and travel in each day in their own carriages. The poor could only live within walking distance of their work, which at this time could have been between three to four miles away. The introduction of horse-drawn omnibuses in 1829 did not help much as their fares were high. A journey from Paddington to the Bank, for instance, cost 1s (5p — a small fortune at the time). Long distance travellers used stagecoaches which ran to London from all the major towns and cities in this country. What is particularly interesting is that, in a survey of public transport travel patterns taken in 1863, only one person in four was using the railway. It seems the remainder still preferred to use river steamers or horse cabs. Certainly, whilst the travelling public were reasonably well served, the supply of food and fuel into London had always caused a problem. Roads in and out of the capital were in a very poor state and many of the commodities had to be transported over long distances. For example much of the coal came from the northeast; grain, cattle and livestock came from the southwest, Wales or even Scotland, and thus journeys must have been extremely long and arduous.

This situation was partially alleviated with the construction of the first canals. These were built to give access to both the city and its docks. The first of these was the Grand Junction Canal, which ran from the industrial Midlands and opened through to Paddington on 21 June 1801. The Regents Canal, which was opened some years later, improved the transport of northeast coal from the docks (where it had been brought by ship) to the city. Several other 'local' canals were constructed to link the docks with the adjacent rural areas. For many centuries the Thames had provided a source of trade to and from London, with ships unloading their cargo at the many small wharves and jetties situated along the riverbank. However, it was not until between 1805 and 1830 that proper docks were constructed.

One of the more important of the long distance canals was the Kennet & Avon, completed in 1810, which linked the docks at Bristol, which were opened in 1809, with the Thames at Reading. Although the ease of journey was infinitely better on the canals than the roads, and much heavier loads could be carried by canal, this form of transport was not without its problems. For instance, a particularly dry summer would see many of the canals made unnavigable due to the shortage of water whilst in the winter severe weather would see the canals freeze up sometimes for weeks on end. It was against these problems that many of the railways into London, and the Great Western in particular, were constructed.

Class 47 No 47582 *County of Norfolk* prepares to depart from Paddington with the 00.50 newspaper train to Bristol Temple Meads on 16 January 1988. Newspaper trains were withdrawn during July 1988 when this traffic was switched to road transport. *Brian Beer*

3. The Growth of the Great Western Railway in London

In telling the story of the opening of the line between Paddington and Twyford, mention must be made of the Kennet and Avon Canal, for the construction of this waterway is closely linked to the formation of the Great Western Railway itself.

From as early as Elizabethan times various schemes had been suggested to link the Avon with the Thames but it was not until 22 May 1712 that the Avon Navigation Bill was passed for the purpose of 'the clearing making and effecting a passage for Boats, Lighters, and other Vessels on the River Avon between Hanham Mills (Bristol) and Bath'. Work on this first section started in April 1724 and was completed and ready to open on 15 December 1727. The second stage of the link, to improve the Kennet between Reading and Newbury, received Royal Assent on 21 September 1715 and was completed on 1 June 1723. The final link, the Western Canal, was proposed by the newly-formed Kennet & Avon Canal Co in 1770. Work was started under the control of engineer John Rennie in October 1774, and the canal was finally completed and open for through navigation over the 86½ miles between Reading and Hanham Mills on 31 December 1810.

Plan of Great Western Railway dated 1835. *Great Western Trust*

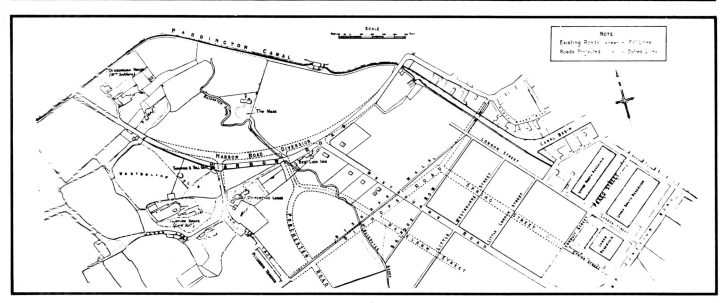

Map showing proposed site of Paddington Station dated 1837. *Great Western Trust*

The new canal now allowed a direct link from the docks at Bristol to those in London and more importantly was a much cheaper carrier than road haulage. The canal itself was initially very successful, taking vast amounts of traffic away from the roads. It must be remembered that at this time road transport of any kind was painfully slow and very costly, since goods were carried in small amounts using carts along what were essentially dirt tracks. It is worth mentioning that until the establishment of toll roads in 1695 the roads in Britain were generally considered to be the worst in Europe. These toll roads soon became known as Turnpike Roads because of the horizontal spiked barrier turning on a post to form a toll gate. Turnpike roads were not only expensive to use but also soon fell into a poor state of repair. The slow progress of road transport was aggravated by the fact that most livestock was moved 'on the hoof'. It is not hard to imagine the problems that this caused in wet weather.

The new canal now allowed much larger quantities of commodities to be moved between Bristol and London at a much cheaper rate. What at first seemed to be an ideal method of transport soon encountered problems for, during a severe winter, the canal would freeze up, suspending traffic for days on end. The summer months also brought their own problems when a particularly dry spell would cause low water levels in the canal. It was, however, the Thames itself that caused many of the navigation problems with low water levels in the summer and flooding in the winter. One might be forgiven for thinking that in our climate low water levels on the Thames were an infrequent occurrence but records show that it happened almost every year, sometimes closing stretches of the river for weeks at a time. In November 1814, for instance, a Reading newspaper reported that, because of low water levels in the

Thames, no boats from London had been able get through for over a month and that goods were being unloaded at Reading and sent on to London by road. The report also states that the waggoners employed to do the carrying were charging up to three times the normal water rate.

To the merchants of Bristol, Reading and London these must have been frustrating times and it was against this background that the Great Western Railway was formed.

Probably the first idea of a rail link between the two cities came with the promotion of the London & Bristol Rail Road Co in 1824. One of the directors of this company was one John McAdam, who at this time was also the surveyor of the Bristol Turnpike. With his experience of road building he was soon

appointed to be the railway's engineer. Interestingly, the route that he planned, which ran via Mangotsfield, Wootton Bassett and the Vale of the White Horse, was not unlike Brunel's route of 1835. However, the scheme proved to be both over-ambitious and costly and soon passed into history. One year later, in 1825, a proposal was made by a group of Kennet & Avon Canal shareholders for a railway from London to Reading, with the object of using the canal to convey goods to the West of England, but once again this came to nothing.

Our story now moves on to a small office in Temple Backs, Bristol. It was here, in August 1832, that four Bristol businessmen, George Jones, John Harford, Thomas Guppy and William Tothill, held an informal meeting and agreed to resurrect the idea of a Bristol-London Railway. By the time the first official meeting was held in January 1833 the new committee had increased to 15 members. At that meeting it was agreed to provide funds for a preliminary survey and to appoint an engineer. The man they chose (on 7 March 1833) was the 27-year old engineer to the Bristol Dock Co and the designer of the Clifton suspension bridge — Isambard Kingdom Brunel.

Together with William Townsend, a land surveyor, Brunel undertook a hasty survey of the country between London and Bristol. This was completed by the middle of June; the proposed route of the new railway would run via Chippenham, Swindon, the Vale of the White Horse and the Thames Valley, with the cost of construction estimated at £2,800,000. The report was submitted and accepted at a meeting in Bristol on 30 July 1833 when the following resolution was passed: 'a company should

---

GREAT WESTERN RAILWAY.

The Public are informed that this Railway will be opened for the conveyance of Passengers only, between London, West Drayton, Slough, and Maidenhead on MONDAY the 4th June. The following will be the times for the departure of Trains each way, from London and from Maidenhead, excepting on Sundays, until further notice.

Trains Each Way.

8 o'clock, Morning.   4 o'clock, Afternoon.
9   ,,   ,,   5   ,,   ,,
10   ,,   ,,   6   ,,   ,,
12   ,,   ,,   7   ,,   ,,

No persons can be admitted to the Carriages without delivering a Ticket. Tickets may be obtained, on payment of the Company's Fares, at the CROWN INN, SLOUGH, subject to there being room in the Carriages on the arrival of the Train.

By Order of the Directors,

Chas. A. Saunders } *Secretaries.*
Thos. Osler

Timetable as published in London *Times* May 1838. *Great Western Trust*

Photography as we know it today was not available in the 1830s and 1840s so many of the following illustrations are artists' impressions and although reasonably accurate do contain a bit of artistic licence. This artist's impression shows the general layout at Paddington in c1840. On the left is the Bishop's Road bridge and the station entrance. Closer inspection shows a coach entering the station through an arch of the bridge. In the foreground and to the right is the goods yard and the large wooden goods shed. *Great Western Trust*

be formed for the establishment of railway communications between Bristol and London, and for that purpose a body of directors for Bristol be appointed, who, in conjunction with a similar body to be appointed in London, shall constitute a general board of management for succouring subscriptions and obtaining an act of parliament for effecting the same object.'

On 19 August 1833 at the offices of Anthony Gibb & Sons at Lime Street in London the newly-formed Bristol & London committee met and adopted the name 'The Great Western Railway'. The prospectus for the new railway offered subscribers the chance to invest in the new company at a cost of £100 per share with the intention of raising the £3,000,000 required to construct the line.

With capital slow to materialise the Bill that was deposited with Parliament in November 1833 was for only the partial construction of the line: from Vauxhall Bridge to Reading; a branch from Slough to Windsor; and the section from Bristol to Bath. It was envisaged that powers to complete the 70-mile section between Reading and Bath could be obtained as and when the money was raised.

Strong objections to the Bill came from many sources including the Provost and Masters of Eton College who stated, amongst other things, that if the new railway were built then the 'boys would, by its aid, seek the doubtful dissipation of town, and so injure

their morals before their absence could be detected by the college authorities'. As a result, the Windsor branch was dropped from the Bill in February 1834! Another notable objector was Robert Palmer, the MP for Reading, who did not like the proposed tunnel under his land at Holme Park. (For the 1835 Bill Brunel decided to alter the route and do away with the tunnel.) Another change was to drop the idea of terminating the line near Vauxhall Bridge. The use of Vauxhall Bridge as a terminus would have required the GWR to construct a 24ft-high viaduct with a 6ft 6in-high parapet 'to prevent passengers looking into dwellers' homes'. On 10 March 1834 the Bill had its second reading in the House of Commons and, after a lengthy debate, it was passed. The examination committee for the Bill under the chairmanship of Lord Granville Somerset first met on 16 April and took 57 days to hear all the evidence for and against the the new railway. Much of the evidence submitted in support of the construction of the line was centred on the excessive time and cost of using canals, roads and rivers for the transport of goods. Support for the

project also came in other unusual ways; one example being from a Bristol wine merchant who complained that beer and spirits conveyed by canal were 'being pilfered or adulterated en route'. This latter reference was to a process which was known as 'sucking the monkey', which entailed unlawfully removing some of the contents of bottles or barrels and replacing it with either water or some other substance. One can only speculate what the latter might have been! The slow journey times on the canal were also quoted in defence of the railway, but a Thames Surveyor stated that he considered that the normal journey time of between two and three days to be 'quite ample for all the purposes of commerce' and that the delays 'were generally caused by the barge men going on shore and getting intoxicated and not minding their own

This lithograph shows the entrance to the terminus itself. The Bishop's Road bridge is on the right. In the background is the Prince of Wales Hotel. Part of the station can be seen on the left. *Great Western Trust*

Another view of the same scene by a different artist shows the parcels platform. Great Western Trust

secretary, Charles Saunders, was able to announce that all the share issue had been taken up and that the Bill had been presented to Parliament. Interestingly, prior to the submission of this Bill, Brunel had persuaded Lord Shaftesbury, who was Chairman of Committees in the House of Lords, to allow the omission of a clause specifying the gauge of the railway. For a number of years Brunel had been thinking about using a wider gauge than 4ft 8½in although at this time he did not specify a particular width.

On 9 March 1835 the Bill had its second reading in the Commons and was passed without opposition. In the House of Lords the Bill was read for the first time on 28 May and, on 10 June 1835, it

business and there was no occasion whatever from a commercial point of view for a railway between London and Reading'.

Despite all the objections, on the 57th day of the hearing the committee gave their approval. However, the euphoria of the company was to be short-lived for, on 25 July, the Bill was rejected by the House of Lords on the ground that the bill offered no security for the completion of the whole line between London and Bristol.

Undaunted, in September the directors issued a supplementary prospectus to try and raise a further £2,000,000, the sum which was needed to construct the line throughout.

In November 1834 yet another prospectus was issued, for a 114-mile long line 'commencing at or near a certain field called Temple Mead within the parish of Temple otherwise Holy Cross in the City and County of the City of Bristol, adjoining or near to the new cattle market there', passing through specified parishes in the Counties of Gloucester, Somerset, Wilts, Berks, Oxford, Bucks and Middlesex, 'and terminating by a Junction with the London and Birmingham Railway in a certain field lying between the Paddington Canal and the Turnpike Road leading from London to Harrow on the western side of the General Cemetery in the Parish or Township of Hammersmith in the said County of Middlesex. The station for passengers in London is intended to be near the New Road in the Parish of St Pancras'. This latter reference was to the London & Birmingham station at Euston.

This time the company were more successful and on 27 February 1835 the

The first published timetable, dated April 1839. Great Western Trust

---

Great Western Railway.

LONDON TO MAIDENHEAD.

On and after the 1st of May, the SOUTHALL STATION will be opened

For Passengers and Parcels.

An **Extra Train** to **Slough** will leave Paddington on **Sunday Mornings**, at **half-past 9 o'clock**, calling at Ealing, Hanwell, Southall and West Drayton.

Horses and Carriages, being at the Paddington or Maidenhead Station ten minutes before the departure of a Train, will be conveyed upon this Railway.

Charge for 4-wheel Carriage, 12s.   Two-wheel ditto, 8s.   For 1 Horse, 10s.   Pair of Horses, 16s.

Post Horses are kept in readiness both at Paddington and Maidenhead, and upon sufficient notice being given at Paddington, or at the Bull and Mouth Office, St. Martin's-le-Grand, would be sent to bring Carriages from any part of London to the station, at a moderate charge.

TRAINS.

From Paddington To Maidenhead.		From Maidenhead To Paddington.	
8 o'clock morn. calling at	- Southall and Slough	6 o'clock morning, calling at	- - Slough
9 do.	- - Slough		(and on Wednesday Morning at Southall)
10 do.	West Drayton and Slough	8 do.	- Slough and West Drayton
12 do.	West Drayton and Slough	9 do.	- Slough and West Drayton
2 o'clock afternoon	West Drayton and Slough	10 do.	- - Slough and Southall
4 do.	- - Slough	12 do.	Slough and West Drayton
5 do.	- Hanwell and Slough	2 o'clock afternoon	- Slough and Southall
6 o'clock evening	Ealing, West Drayton and Slough	4 do.	- - Slough
7 do.	- Southall and Slough	5 do.	- Slough and Hanwell
8 do.	- - Slough	6 o'clock evening	Slough and West Drayton
		7 do.	- Slough and Ealing

The six o'clock up Train will call at Southall on Wednesday mornings, for the convenience of persons attending the market on that day.

SHORT TRAINS.

From Paddington To West Drayton.		From West Drayton To Paddington.	
¼ past 9 o'Clock Morning,		¼ before 9 o'Clock Morning,	
½ past 1 do. Afternoon,	calling at { Ealing, Hanwell, AND Southall.	¼ before 11 do.	calling at { Southall, Hanwell, AND Ealing.
¼ past 4 do. do.		½ before 3 Afternoon	
¼ past 8 do. Evening		¼ before 7 o'Clock Evening	

☞ *There are no second class close carriages in the short Trains.*

Passengers and Parcels for Slough and Maidenhead will be conveyed from all the stations by means of the short Trains, waiting to be taken on by the succeeding long Train, as above; and in like manner they will be conveyed from Maidenhead and Slough, to every station on the Line.

On SUNDAYS,

From Paddington To Maidenhead.		From Maidenhead To Paddington.	
8 o'clock Morn, calling at	- Ealing and Slough	6 o'clock morn, calling at	- - - Slough
¼ past 9 do. do.	West Drayton and Slough	8 do. do.	Slough Southall and Ealing
5 afternoon do.	Southall and Slough	9 do.	Slough West Drayton and Hanwell
6 evening do.	Hanwell West Drayton and Slough	5 afternoon do.	- - Slough and Hanwell
7 do. do.	Ealing West Drayton and Slough	6 evening do.	- Slough and West Drayton
	- Southall and Slough	7 do. do.	- Slough and Ealing

SHORT TRAINS, PADDINGTON TO SLOUGH.

Half-past Nine o'Clock Morning, - - - calling at **Ealing, Hanwell, Southall, and Drayton.**

To West Drayton.		From West Drayton.	
¼ past 9 o'Clock Morning, calling at {	Ealing, Hanwell, & Southall. and proceeding to Slough	¼ before 8 o'Clock Morning, calling at {	Southall, Hanwell & Ealing.
¼ past 8 do. Evening,	Ealing, Hanwell & Southall	¼ before 7 do. Evening,	

FARES.

Paddington.	1st. Class. Coach.	Second Class. Close.	Open.	Maidenhead.	1st. Class. Coach.	Second Class. Close.	Open.
To Ealing	1 6	1 0	0 9	To Slough	2 0	1 6	1 0
Hanwell ...	2 0	1 6	1 0	West Drayton	3 0	2 6	2 0
Southall	2 6	1 9	1 3	Southall	4 0	3 0	2 6
West Drayton	3 6	2 0	1 6	Hanwell ...	4 6	3 6	3 0
Slough	4 6	3 0	2 6	Ealing	5 0	4 0	3 6
Maidenhead .	5 6	4 0	3 6	Paddington .	5 6	4 0	3 6

A painting showing the rural atmosphere of Ealing Haven (Broadway) station in the 1840s. *Great Western Trust*

received its second reading and this time it was carried by a vote of 46 to 34. The subsequent inquiry, headed by Lord Wharncliffe, heard evidence for and against the railway with many of the objections being centred on the potential dangers of the steep gradient through Box Tunnel with such outbursts as 'monstrous, extraordinary, dangerous and impractical'. With the use of models Brunel demonstrated that these rather hysterical objections were unfounded and, after 40 days of deliberation, the committee found in favour of the railway. On 28 August the Bill was sent for its third reading after which it received Royal Assent on 31 August 1835.

And so the Great Western Railway was born.

The task in hand now was actually to construct the line. The omission of the gauge clause from the Act now allowed Brunel to consider the gauge of the line and, in a report to the company on 15 September 1835, he proposed a gauge width of between 6ft 10in and 7ft. One of the main obstacles to using this gauge was removed, when, owing to a disagreement with the London & Birmingham Railway over land rights, the proposal to terminate the line at Euston was abandoned and, instead, it was decided to extend the line from Acton to 'a certain space of ground adjoining the basin of the Paddington Canal in the parish of Paddington'. The canal here was the Paddington Branch of the Grand Junction Canal. The Grand Junction had been opened between the

Thames, at Brentford, and Weedon on 21 June 1796. The Paddington arm was opened on 10 July 1801. In 1929 the Grand Junction became part of the Grand Union Canal with the amalgamation of the Grand Junction, the Warwick & Napton and the Warwick & Birmingham Canals. A glance at the modern Ordnance Survey map of the Old Oak Common area shows, to this day, the obvious change of route to Paddington.

At a meeting of the GWR board on 29 October 1835 Brunel's 7ft gauge was adopted. The construction of the 18-mile section between Acton and the temporary terminus at Maidenhead started almost immediately. However, work on the 4½-mile section from Acton to Paddington was delayed until the Act for this section was passed on 3 July 1837. This provided for the northwards deviation of the Harrow Road, near the Westbourne turnpike gate, and the making of sundry bridges, including a wide road bridge in place of the existing footbridge over the Paddington Canal

close to the intended depot of the railway and over the railway itself from Harrow Road to Spring Street, whence a new road was to be made by the company, in lieu of the footpath known as Bishop's Walk, to Black Lion Lane. One unexpected, but tiresome, consequence of the delay in obtaining Parliamentary authority for the diversion to Paddington was that, in 1836, the Birmingham, Bristol & Thames Junction Railway was empowered to cross the line of the intended GW main line on the level at a point later known as West London Junction. As will be seen, this was later to cause the GWR considerable difficulties.

The first contract to be let went to Messrs Grissell and Peto and was for the construction of the viaduct across the Brent Valley at Hanwell. Work

This painting shows the up and down stations at Slough in c1841. *Great Western Trust*

in March 1839, when, under the excessive weight, one of the girders gave way. Brunel's answer was to lighten the load by removing the brick arches and replacing them with wooden planks. This seemed to do the trick but, in May 1847, the planks caught fire, probably from a passing engine, and the ensuing heat severely damaged the cast-iron structure of the bridge. It was subsequently rebuilt by Brunel, this time using wrought-iron.

By August 1837 much of the work was complete although no track had yet been laid. Brunel had considered the design of the track carefully and eventually decided to use longitudinal timbers, which would be stabilised by a series of cross timbers or transoms held in place by beech piles driven into the ground. The track itself weighed 43lb to the yard and because of its shape was known as bridge rail.

In June 1837 Brunel appointed Daniel Gooch as the GW's first locomotive Superintendent. Gooch, who was 21 when he entered service on 18 August 1838, had to wait until November before the first two engines, *Vulcan* and *Premier*, were delivered, by canal, to West Drayton. It was here that the first locomotive headquarters was set up. A small engine shed was constructed together with some coke ovens, since these early engines burnt coke, not coal.

The initial progress in track laying was slow: a report of 12 April 1838 states that only 5¾ miles had been laid. Gradually the line began to take shape and by the middle of May it was almost complete.

began in February 1836 and was finished in August 1837. The 896ft long viaduct, which is designed by Brunel, cost £40,000 to construct. The whole structure, which is built of brick, contains eight 70ft span arches and stands 65ft above the valley. (The river Brent actually runs beneath the second eastern arch.) Originally the viaduct was just 30ft wide but the provision of an additional track between Paddington and West Drayton in 1861 saw the viaduct widened to 52ft. In August 1837 it was officially named the 'Wharncliffe Viaduct' in recognition of Lord Wharncliffe, a great supporter of the company, who was also the chairman of the Committee on the Act of Incorporation of the Company in the House of Lords in 1835. Its construction presented problems for Brunel because the embankments at either side of the viaduct suffered from severe sloping due to the nature of the clay. In November 1837 Brunel reported that 'the daily settlement of the embankments at Hanwell which had gradually diminished in amount and

apparently from the good effects of the remedies which had been applied, have within the last few days somewhat increased in amount (this was 1½in in 24hr) and that after careful examination of the ground with the contractors and their principal managing men it appeared that the most certain and effectual means as well as the most easy of application would be to increase the spread and weight of the terraces which have been formed on the north side as a counterweight or balance to the embankment and the contractor has commenced carting gravel for that purpose'.

Another obstacle lay just to the east of the viaduct where the line crossed the main Uxbridge/Brentford and Greenford roads at an angle of 45°. Here Brunel designed a cast-iron 'skew' girder bridge. The method of construction used a combination of cast-iron girders in-filled with flat arches of bricks. This was an unusual method of construction and the bridge must have been extremely heavy, a fact borne out

14

For the London terminus the company had obtained a large quantity of land from the Bishop of London. It was Brunel's original intention to construct a permanent station at Paddington but, because of the time factor in trying to open the line as soon as possible, he built a temporary station to the east of the Bishop's Road Bridge. This station is described in detail in a later chapter.

Incidentally, I have found two possible explanations as to the origin of the name 'Padynton' (original spelling). The first is derived from the manor or estate of the De Padinton family as recorded by Abbot Walter of Westminster in 1191. The second suggests that in Saxon times the Paeda family (ing) established a homestead (ton) here.

During May 1838 the 22½-mile section between Paddington and a temporary station at Maidenhead was at last ready for use. This first station was actually situated one mile east of Maidenhead at the Dumb Bell Bridge, Taplow. This was no arbitrary decision to place the first terminus at this point for, in 1834, the GW had commissioned a census of traffic passing along the Bath Road and, in order to tap some of this traffic, had constructed the station adjacent to the bridge that carried the new railway over the Bath Road. It is interesting to note that the GWR magazine refers to a set of stone steps that were removed from this station in 1845

and re-erected at the Bishop's Road bridge 'so that passengers might approach more closely to the Paddington Station booking office'.

On 31 May an experimental run for invited guests, who included directors of the railway and MPs, was made in anticipation of the opening of the new railway. The special train, which left Paddington at 11 o'clock, contained six coaches and was hauled by the engine *North Star*. Brunel himself was on the footplate, and the 22½-mile journey was completed in 49min. On Whit Monday, 4 June 1838, the first section of the GWR was finally opened to the public. The first train, which was again hauled by the engine *North Star*, left Paddington at 8am with about 200 passengers on board. Newspaper reports indicate that the train attained a maximum speed of 36mph, and G. H. Gibbs, a director of the company, noted in his diary 'Our railway opened to the public this morning. I went to Maidenhead by the first train and came back by the third, which started from Maidenhead

at 10.15. I was disappointed with regard to the speed, as we were 1 hour and 20 minutes going down and 1 hour and 5 minutes coming up. If from the 65 minutes we deduct 4 lost at Drayton, 3 at Slough, and 4 between the two places in slackening and getting up speed, there remain 54 minutes for 23 miles or 25½ miles per hour. We carried altogether today 1,479 people and took £226.'

A particularly interesting feature of the new railway was the provision of the first working electric telegraph. The system used by the GW was designed by Cooke and Wheatstone and was installed between Paddington and West

The up Royal luggage train hauled by Great Western 4-2-2 No 3040 *Empress of India*, pictured here near Acton on 21 June 1897. *Great Western Trust*

Drayton in time for the opening. It was later extended to Slough.

According to the GW magazine the Great Western's first engine driver was Jim Hurst. He had entered the company's employ in August 1837 and, for several months after the opening of the line, became the regular driver of the 8am service from Paddington.

Travelling between Paddington and Taplow today it is difficult to imagine the rural nature of the route at that time but an indication can be gleaned from this passenger's description of that first journey that was published in the *Reading Mercury* all those years ago: 'The route taken was then by Hanwell, Southall and Drayton, through a beautifully wooded and fertile district, and the sudden transformation from the smoke, dust and noise of London to the quiet glades and umbrageous thickets of the park-like country we were then traversing, appeared more like the work of magic than the result of the ingenuity and labour of man'.

Opening services show eight trains a day in each direction on weekdays and six on Sundays. There was only one intermediate station, at West Drayton, although trains were advertised to stop at Slough where there was no station. The reason for this strange state of affairs was that the 1835 Bill precluded the company from constructing any station or depot within three miles of Eton College without prior permission of the Provost. The GW's answer was to divert an existing road closer to the railway and to stop the trains adjacent to the road. Initially, two rooms were hired at the nearby Crown Hotel for use as a booking office but, from 20 September 1838, booking was undertaken from the 'North Star' public house which had been opened only a few yards from the line. The College soon sought an injunction to stop the company advertising

Slough as a stop, but after many months of wrangling common sense prevailed and the College backed down.(A station was eventually opened at Slough on 4 June 1841.) What is extraordinary about all of this is that even as the wrangling was going on many officials and students of the College were actively using the railway to travel to and from the College!

During the first 10 weeks of operation the new railway carried 100,222 passengers, producing receipts of £15,974.

Further stations were opened at Ealing and Hanwell in December 1838 and at Southall on 1 May 1839. Although work on the section between Maidenhead and Twyford had started in 1837 it was not until 1 July 1839 that this section was opened for traffic. The delay was mainly caused by the construction of the bridge across the Thames at Maidenhead. The Thames Commissioners had stipulated to Brunel that the new bridge must in no way obstruct the navigation channel or the towpath. Therefore, to cross the river which is nearly 100yd wide here, Brunel designed a flat arched bridge, in brick, with two main spans of 128ft with a rise of only 24ft 3in. The two main arches were flanked at either end by four smaller ones to provide for the passage of flood water.It was certainly one of the most remarkable bridges ever constructed. The contract to construct the bridge was let to the firm of Chadwick's of London. Work was started on the bridge and the surrounding embankments in the spring of 1837 and, by February 1838, the directors were able to report that the work was in an advanced state. Critics of the design declared that with such flat arches the bridge would collapse. In May 1838 the centerings supporting the brickwork were eased, and although the western arch was satisfactory, some distortion appeared on the eastern arch. As it turned out it was not Brunel who was at fault, but the contractors. They admitted liability stating that they had eased the centering before the mortar had set. The faulty brickwork was repaired and the centerings were again eased some months later. On 12 April 1839 a special test train crossed the bridge and although it stood firm Brunel decided to leave the centerings in place for another winter. However, during a severe storm the centres were blown down, leaving the arches standing. Apparently Brunel had already had

Between 1910 and 1914 a number of the old brick road bridges between Paddington and Acton were rebuilt. This before and after pair of pictures shows the Lord's Hill Bridge at Royal Oak, which was reconstructed in 1914. *Great Western Trust*

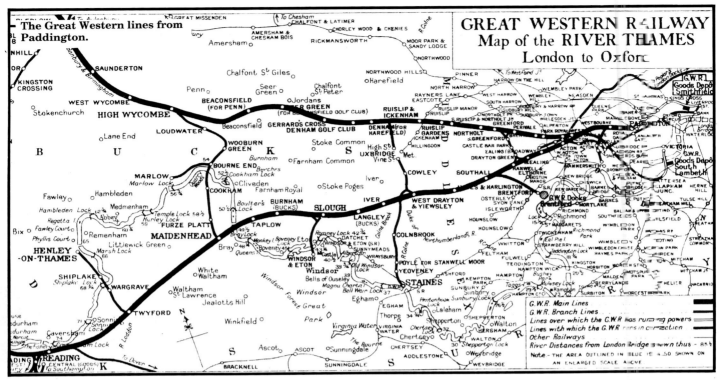

The Great Western lines from Paddington.

GREAT WESTERN RAILWAY
Map of the RIVER THAMES
London to Oxford

the centres eased and therefore knew all along that the bridge would stand.

On 1 July 1839 the line was opened through to Twyford. Owing to the difficulties with the construction of Sonning Cutting (explained in my book *Rail Centres: Reading*), Twyford became the terminus of the line for almost a year. The first station at Twyford was a temporary wooden structure, which comprised a single platform on the up side of the line. The station building was a rather unusual 'T'-shape and stood at right angles to the platform. The attractive stone station at Twyford was not

constructed until 1845. Early plans of Twyford also show a large wooden shed, which straddled the tracks at the west end of the station and was probably used for storing stock. It is quite possible that this building was removed from the Dumb Bell Bridge station at Maidenhead and re-erected at Twyford.

Because of the problems with Sonning, the GW, together with other carriers, operated a connecting coach service between the station at Twyford and Reading. However, the problems at Sonning were eventually overcome and the line was opened through to Reading on

30 March 1840, to Chippenham on 31 May 1841 and to Bristol on 30 June 1841. A major feature of the new railway was that between Paddington and Didcot the line was, to all intents and purposes, built on the level.

Passengers wait patiently as an up local service arrives at West Ealing in 1916. Because of width restrictions, the up relief platform (seen here) was constructed to the east of the main station. *Great Western Trust*

Expansion

The railway infrastructure in the Great Western's London division was extended with the opening of various branch lines. The earliest of these was the Slough & Windsor Railway which opened on 3 October 1849. This was followed by the Wycombe Railway's branch from Maidenhead to High Wycombe on 1 August 1853. Other branches were opened between West Drayton and Uxbridge on 8 September 1856, Twyford and Henley on 1 June 1857, Southall and Brentford on 18 July 1859 and finally between West Drayton and Staines on 2 November 1885. These are covered in more detail in the chapter on branch lines.

Yet another important opening was the junction between the Great Western and the West London Railway at West London Junction and North Pole on 1 April 1863. This junction, together with the opening West London Extension Railway, gave the GW an important through connection to the south of the capital. The GW also had joint interests in both the Metropolitan Railway, which opened between Bishop's Road and Farringdon on 10 January 1863, and the Hammersmith & City line, which opened between Bishop's Road and Hammersmith on 13 June 1864.

The next major step forward in the development of the line in the Thames Valley was the quadrupling of the track between Westbourne Park and West Drayton to provide a separate pair of

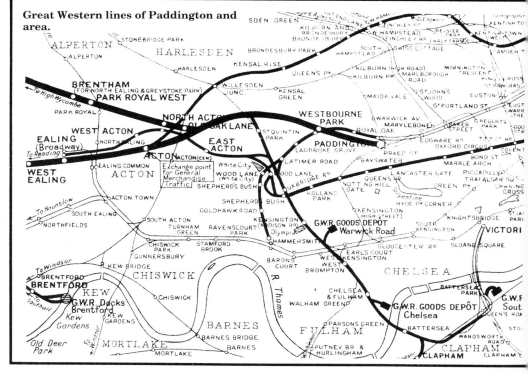

Great Western lines of Paddington and area.

The attractive station at Hanwell and Elthorne in 1919. *L&GRP*

slow lines. The term 'main' line and 'relief' line was not officially adopted by the Great Western Railway until 1 January 1880.

Work on the construction of the new lines was started in 1874 and progressed slowly. Part of the problem was, of course, the need to widen Wharncliffe Viaduct and the associated embankments. However, so good was the original Brunel design that the new viaduct section was built to match the original exactly. The new relief lines, which were built to the standard gauge, were extended westwards in various stages,

opening between Portobello Junction and Southall on 1 October 1877, Southall-West Drayton on 25 November 1878, West Drayton-Slough on 1 June 1879 and from Slough to Taplow on 8 September 1884. It was during this time that many of the original stations, which had initially been constructed to accommodate two tracks, were also rebuilt.

The work of doubling the section between Taplow, Reading and Didcot was not started until the summer of 1890. The work was to be made slightly easier with the decision, in 1891, to

A GW 4-4-0 heads an up service through Slough in 1912. Notice the East signal cabin, set at right angles against the platform. *Great Western Trust*

remove all remaining broad and mixed gauge tracks by the summer of the following year; this latter task was completed, of course, during the weekend of 21/22 May 1892.

Apart from widening various cuttings and embankments, one of the major tasks on this section involved the widening of Maidenhead Bridge. The bridge itself received special attention with the original yellow bricks being replaced by a more expensive red brick from Cattybrook near Bristol. As with the Wharncliffe Viaduct, the new section of bridge was built to match Brunel's original design.

The new relief lines were once again opened in various sections first as goods loops, but then to passenger traffic between Didcot and Moulsford on 27 December 1892, Maidenhead-Reading on 4 June 1893 and from Reading West Junction to Pangbourne on 30 July 1893. The new layout now gave the GW, apart from a short section through Reading yard that was not completed until 1899, a four-track railway all the way from Westbourne Park to Didcot.

It was around this time that the GW was considering constructing a shorter route to Birmingham. The old route, via Reading and Oxford, gave the company a distinct disadvantage in both time and mileage over its rival — the LNWR. One such proposal envisaged an upgrading of the old Wycombe Railway route to form a new main line via Princes Risborough, Thame and Oxford,

but as will be seen, this scheme was not adopted.

From the start, the Great Central who were having problems with the Metropolitan Railway over running rights between Aylesbury and Marylebone, had shown great interest in the project and on 1 August 1899 they linked up with the GWR to form a joint committee to construct and administer the new route.

Authorised by Acts of 1897 and 1905 the construction of the line was divided into three parts. The sections between Old Oak and Northolt and Ashendon-Aynho were the GW's responsibility, with the centre section, between Northolt and Ashendon, the responsibility of the Great Western & Great Central Joint Committee. Work on the southern section, between Old Oak Common West Junction and Northolt, was started in 1901 and was opened as far as Park Royal on 15 June 1903. Greenford was reached on 1 October 1904 and on 2 April 1906 the line was opened through to Grendon Underwood. The GCR's own connection between Northolt and Neasden was opened on 1 March 1906.

By this time the GW had abandoned its idea of upgrading the route via

Thame and, instead, decided to construct a new line northwards from Princes Risborough, across the Vale of Aylesbury, to join the Oxford-Birmingham line at Aynho. This section was opened for passenger traffic on 1 July 1910 and was actually the last main line to be built in this country until the building of the Selby diversion and was engineered to the highest standards with passing loops being provided at many of the stations.

The 1897 Act also provided for the construction of a 2½-mile loop line connecting Greenford, on the new line, with West Ealing on the old. The 'Greenford loop' was opened for passenger traffic on 23 June 1903. The first services over the new loop conveyed passengers to the Royal Agricultural Show at Park Royal. Intermediate stations were opened at Castle Bar Park Halt on 1 May 1904, at Drayton Green on 1 March 1905 and at South Greenford on 20 September 1926.

During 1908 the company obtained powers to reconstruct 10 of the old overbridges between Acton and Paddington. Many of these dated from the opening of the railway and were constructed of brick. The Bishop's Road and Ranelagh bridges, for example, each contained nine brick arches. Both were replaced during 1909 with massive steel girder structures. Ranelagh bridge was completed in July and Bishop's Road in December.

Railway development on the GW in the London area finally came with the completion of two electric lines. The

Passengers waiting on the up main platform at West Drayton & Yiewsley Station c1920. *Great Western Trust*

first was the Ealing & Shepherd's Bush railway, which was opened for goods traffic on 16 April 1917. This 4¾-mile branch was authorised in 1905 and connected Ealing with the new line at North Acton, the Central London Railway at Wood Lane Junction, and the West London line near Latimer Road. The original idea, that the branch would run into a terminus station at Shepherd's Bush, was abandoned and, instead, in 1911 the Central London Railway was authorised to extend its own line and make a connection with the branch at Wood Lane. The branch was subsequently electrified and

worked by the Central London Railway, which commenced passenger services between Ealing Broadway and Liverpool Street on 3 August 1920.

In 1936 the Ealing & Shepherd's Bush Railway Extension Act was passed. This Act was jointly promoted by the London Passenger Transport Board, the GW and the LNER for an 11-mile extension of the Central Line from North Acton through to Denham. The

section between Wood Lane and North Acton was quadrupled by the GW in 1937. The second stage of the work which had reached Greenford was curtailed in June 1940 due to the outbreak of war. Construction did not resume until March 1946 but, by this time, a decision had been made to terminate the new line at Ruislip & Ickenham. Electric services eventually commenced running through to Greenford on 30 June 1947 and to Ruislip on 21 November 1948. New stations were opened at Hanger Lane, Perivale, Greenford, Northolt, South Ruislip and Ruislip Gardens. At Greenford a new spur was constructed to connect the west curve to a bay platform at the new station, thus allowing the Western Region's Greenford-Ealing shuttle service to connect with the new electric services. At Ruislip a large electric rolling stock servicing depot was constructed. The new depot, which was also opened in November 1948, is still in use today. The main shed here is over 1,000ft long and provides stabling and repair facilities for up to 350 coaches.

Developments since nationalisation in 1948 are covered within the following chapters.

Left:
Quite a rare view of Manning, Wardle & Co locomotive No 154 *Isabel* built in 1865 and pictured here during the widening of the GW main line near Maidenhead in about 1890. *B. D. Stoyel*

4. The West London Railway

The Birmingham, Bristol & Thames Junction Railway was incorporated on 21 June 1836 to construct a railway from the Kensington Canal basin at Counters Bridge to the London & Birmingham Railway at Holsden Green (Willesden). The company, which changed its name to West London Railway on 23 July 1840, had started with high hopes, but was eventually taken over by the Great Western and the London & North Western.

It was envisaged that the 2½-mile line would run under the Hammersmith Turnpike road and across Wormwood Scrubs to link with the Great Western main line at West London. From here it would reach Willesden via a tunnel under the Grand Junction Canal. Powers were also obtained to purchase the Kensington Canal to allow the company direct access to the River Thames. As was usual in these early schemes money was slow to materialise. Work on the line was actually started in 1836 but, owing to lack of funds, proceeded slowly and a proposed extension of the line from Kensington to Hyde Park did not

materialise. In February 1840, while the line was still uncompleted, a section near to Wormwood Scrubs was used for a short time by Clegg and Samuda for experiments with their 'Atmospheric System'. The system proved quite successful as noted in the following report: 'That the experiments at Wormwood Scrubs have proved the practicality of giving motion to considerable loads, at a maximum velocity of 40 miles per hour'. However, the whole experiment ended up with animosity between the railway company and the patentees. This resulted in the company ordering Clegg and Sumuda off their land. The dispute dragged on and the plant was not removed until March 1843. The final result of the whole affair saw the railway company having to pay Clegg and Sumuda a settlement of £350.

This old lithograph shows the West London and Great Western level crossing at Mitre Bridge in 1844. *Great Western Trust*

Delays in completing the line were becoming horrendous with finances in a particularly torrid state. The company, however, soldiered on and after much delay the single-track West London Railway line was opened without ceremony on Whit Monday 27 May 1844 with a half-hourly service between Willesden Junction and Kensington. Interestingly, it crossed the GW main line near Mitre Bridge on the level and, for a while, West London services connected with the GW via a small interchange platform. This situation had arisen over a disagreement as to the ownership of the land at this point. Eventually an agreement was reached that the Birmingham, Bristol & Thames Junction Co would surrender its prior rights to the crossing in favour of the GW. The ownership of the land was, however, to remain vested with the owning company 'subject to rights granted to the Great Western Company to maintain the land and work their railway without let or hindrance'. The agreement, which was signed on 2 February 1837, required the GW to

The crossing was removed in October 1860 and replaced by the brick bridge seen in this picture taken in 1905. The brick bridge was replaced by a 200ft span girder bridge in 1906. *Great Western Trust*

'provide also for the sidings, rails, switches and other apparatus at the point of the junction to be kept in repair at the expense of the company and to construct and maintain a station or stopping place at the point of the junction of the two lines, where the transfer of passengers and goods would take place'. From 3 June 1844 the GW agreed to stop three down and two up services at the small interchange platforms. London & Birmingham services also called here from Monday 10 June 1844. From the start passenger traffic over the new line was sparse and with finances at a critical stage, services were withdrawn on 30 November 1844. The line, however, was not closed completely and, under an agreement with the London & Birmingham dated 11 March 1845, continued to be used for goods traffic.

The level crossing at Mitre Bridge was a particularly interesting piece of early railway compromise. The following passage, which is taken from an early history of the line, describes the crossing in some detail: 'North of the

actual crossing, the West London line coming from Willesden as a narrow gauge single line proceeded into a cutting some 16ft deep and 120ft long, until it passed under the Grand Junction Canal by an incline of 1 in 36, where it rose to the point at which, on the level, it crossed the two broad gauge tracks of the Great Western Railway. South of the actual crossing, the narrow gauge became "mixed" gauge to accommodate Great Western traffic. The exchange of traffic from narrow to broad gauge, and vice versa, was effected by a turntable on a separate siding, parallel with the Great Western line, where broad gauge track at right angles led to the point where the broad and narrow gauges merged to become mixed gauge. The tunnel of brickwork was of considerable beauty and workmanship, with a handsome elevation on the south and a collateral corridor adjoining, for use as a footway between the adjacent stations'.

From about 1844 the crossing was protected by signals and, on the West London line, by large wooden barriers

which were lifted using ropes and pulleys. The signals were, at first, not fitted with lamps as the crossing was intended only to be used during daylight hours. For safety reasons, control of the crossing was solely in the hands of the GW. This did not, however, prevent accidents. In April 1850 a GW coal train collided with a derailed West London ballast train on the crossing and in November 1855 a North Western coal train collided with a GW goods train at the same spot. The crossing was obviously a potential danger and as a result the GW obtained powers during 1859 to construct a bridge at this point in order to carry the West London line over its tracks. Work on the project was started almost immediately and was finished in October 1860. Thereafter the old station building at Mitre Bridge was used as a dwelling house and was not finally removed by the GW until 1934. A proper junction between the two lines was not constructed until the summer of 1862 when the GW doubled the West London line and laid broad gauge tracks between Kensington and Victoria. However, the new junction was not opened for passenger traffic until 2 March 1863 when through services between Southall and Victoria were inaugurated. Interestingly, the short link through Mitre Tunnel (beneath the West London line) to North Pole Junction became known over the years as the Victoria Curve.

On 31 July 1854 the West London Railway was jointly leased to the GW and LNWR and, in 1859, the West London Extension Railway was incorporated to construct a line from Kensington to the west end of the London & Crystal Palace Railway at Longhedge Junction. This was a joint venture between the GW, the LNWR, the London & South Western and the London Brighton & South Coast Railway. Passenger services over the West London section had been restored by the LNWR on 2 June 1862 in time for the International Exhibition at Kensington. The new extension railway, which had been built as a mixed gauge line, was opened for passenger services on 2 March 1863. Initially, there were just three intermediate stations — at Kensington, Battersea and Chelsea. Further stations were opened at West Brompton on

Great Western 'Metropolitan' class 2-4-0T No 3567 stands in the goods bay at Kensington Addison Road on 6 February 1932. *E. R. Wethersett*

Ex-South Eastern & Chatham 'C' class 0-6-0 No 31583 runs through Kensington Olympia in 1959 with a short goods comprising just a road tank and a guards van. Kensington South box, which, although closed in late 1992, is currently still standing, can be seen on the right whilst, on the left, a row of milk tanks stand in the milk siding.
J. G. Edwards

1 September 1866, Uxbridge Road on 1 November 1869, and St Quintin Park and Wormwood Scrubs on 1 August 1871. Kensington was renamed Kensington Addison Road in 1868 to avoid confusion with the Metropolitan station at Kensington High Street.

The station at Kensington became very busy with daily services from the GW, the LNWR, the LBSCR and the LSWR. GW passenger services over the line comprised eight a day in each direction between Southall and Victoria. Most of these were standard gauge services. A few broad gauge passenger services ran through to Victoria but these were withdrawn in September 1866. However, broad gauge goods trains (mainly coal) continued to run through to Chelsea Basin until November 1875.

The completion of the line provided an important through route for goods traffic. As already mentioned, the GW's interest centred on the yard at Chelsea Basin. This was situated adjacent to the Thames and was formed by widening the southern end of the old Kensington Canal, parts of which had been filled in to form the trackbed of the railway north of the river. The Kensington Canal had been opened on 12 August 1828 and ran from the Thames to a basin near the Hammersmith Road.

The yard at Chelsea Basin was quite extensive with siding space for several hundred wagons. The goods shed and wharf lines were connected by a series of wagon turntables.

On 1 August 1872 the GW introduced its 'Middle Circle' service from Moorgate to the Mansion House. Outer Circle services were introduced by the LNWR on 1 February 1872 and ran between Broad Street and Mansion House. Both services had been made possible by the construction of two short branches. The first connected the West London with the Hammersmith & City Railway at Uxbridge Road Junction and the second connected the West London with the Metropolitan District line at Earls Court. These services were eventually taken over by the Metropolitan Railway on 1 February 1905 and, from 3 December 1906, were operated using electric traction.

GW services to Victoria were extended and by 1897 were running from Windsor, Reading and Uxbridge. Steam railmotors were introduced on to Greenford-Kensington services in August 1904. From 16 April 1905 the

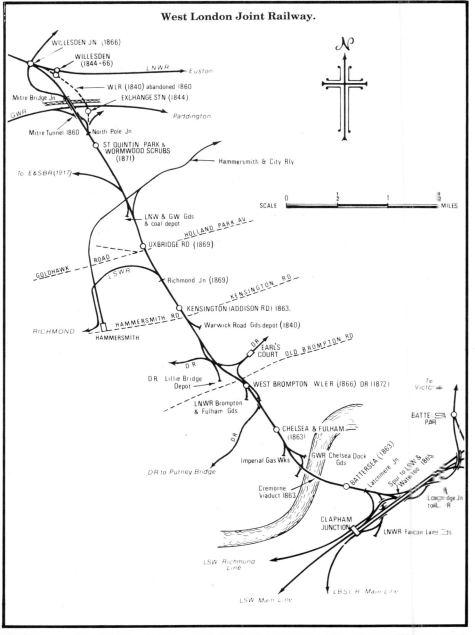

West London Joint Railway.

service was extended with railcars running through to reach Clapham Junction and Victoria. However, with the start of World War 1 the railmotor services were run down and were eventually withdrawn on 22 March 1915. During 1906 the two old brick bridges at Scrubs Lane were replaced by the GW with new 200ft span girder bridges. Interestingly, at this point, the junction line passed under the canal while Scrubs Lane passed over both — a formation repeated on the Brentford branch.

In October 1910 a through service from Victoria to Wolverhampton was inaugurated but with the outbreak of World War 1 many of the services were withdrawn and, on 12 July 1915, GW passenger services over the West London line to Victoria ceased.

The GW was not alone in providing through trains and probably the most famous to use the West London route was the 'Sunny South Express'. This service, which was inaugurated in 1905, ran up until the start of World War 2 and carried through carriages from Liverpool and Manchester to Brighton and Eastbourne.

On 1 May 1914 LNWR services between Willesden Junction and Earls Court were electrified. In 1933 Metropolitan services were taken over

Top:
Class 33 No 33064 passes through Kensington Olympia on 14 February 1977 with an empty ballast train.
David Parker

Above:
Preserved ex-Great Western 2-6-2T No 6106 and a pair of ex-'Bournemouth Belle' Pullman coaches *Isle of Thanet* and *Lydia* stand at Kensington Olympia on 4 November 1967. The engine, which was *en route* to Didcot, also picked up two super saloons Nos 9112 and 9118 from Taplow. The two Pullmans were delivered to Oxford by No 6106 and were eventually shipped to the USA.
Great Western Trust

Today rail services at Kensington are centred on the down side; the old up platform, as can be seen, is closed and unused. Looking down from the road bridge on 16 May 1986 a London Transport service leaves for Kensington High Street as Class 47 No 47444 *University of Nottingham* arrives with the 10.45 service from Dover Western Docks to Liverpool Lime Street. In the background Class 56 No 56061 waits with a down stone train. *Brian Morrison*

and operated jointly by the new London Passenger Transport Board and the GW. During World War 2 the connecting spur between Latimer Road Junction and Uxbridge Road Junction suffered severe bomb damage. LMS services were withdrawn on 3 October 1940. Metropolitan services followed on 21 October, and Southern services to Clapham were also withdrawn from the

same date. Apart from Addison Road itself, all intermediate stations on the line were closed.

After the war the Southern Railway was considering electrifying the line from Longhedge Junction to Addison Road, but the idea was dropped. On 19 December 1946 the station at Addison Road was renamed Kensington Olympia. The large Olympia exhibition

The 13.55 ('Holidaymaker Express') service from Eastbourne to Edinburgh hauled by Class 47 No 47201 passes North Pole Junction signal box on the West London line on 25 June 1988. *Brian Morrison*

hall had been opened during 1886 and, from about 1924, the station was designated 'Kensington (Addison Road) for Olympia'. The lack of passenger traffic over the line was more than made up for with an increase in goods services. During the 1960s the line saw renewed passenger activity firstly during the reconstruction of Euston when, from 1 April 1963 to 15 June 1965, several West Coast services were diverted into Kensington.

On 24 May 1966 a new Motorail terminal was opened, with through services to Perth, St Austell, Fishguard and Newton Abbot. The increased traffic saw a certain amount of modernisation work undertaken on the west side of the station. Between October and November 1967 the West London line saw further use by Western Region passenger services when, during the resignalling work at Paddington, several West of England and Worcester

services started and terminated at Kensington.

From 1 February 1970 control of the West London line was taken over by the London Midland Region. For many years the station at Kensington had been a major centre for milk traffic but this came to an end on 1 May 1972 when the remaining services were diverted to Acton and Clapham.

The Motorail traffic, which had provided such a fillip for the line, declined and was withdrawn from Kensington at the end of the 1982 summer timetable.

Today the West London line still provides an important, if lightly used, through route for freight traffic. Passenger services are, however, sparse and, at Kensington Olympia, the up platform has been closed, with two way working now centred on the down side. The line itself is now under the control of Victoria and, at the time of writing, Kensington South Main signalbox is still standing. The station is currently served by up to three InterCity cross-country services each weekday and locally District Line electrics run a Monday-Saturday shuttle service from Edgware Road or (more often) Kensington High Street and Earls Court with extra exhibition services as required. During 1992 the line between Clapham, Olympia and North Pole was electrified and it is intended that the peak time shuttle service between Olympia and Clapham Junction, currently worked by DMUs, will be operated using Network South-East Electric Multiple-Units from May 1993.

With the introduction of the new Channel Tunnel services empty stock trains from Waterloo will also traverse the line en route to the huge servicing depot at North Pole.

It is hard to imagine, when standing on the platform today, that, at one time, over 200 passenger trains each day were calling at Addison Road.

A view of the refurbished platform at Kensington Olympia on 28 February 1993. Standing at the London Underground bay is a special through 'Exhibition' service to Edgware Road. The South signalbox was closed on 4 October 1992. *Author*

5. The Metropolitan and Hammersmith & City Lines

Passengers arriving at Paddington today have a choice of either bus, taxi or Tube to transport them around the city. Whilst many might use the bus or the taxi, the majority, I think, would use the Tube.

Underground railways first came to Paddington in 1863 with the opening of the Metropolitan line to Farringdon Street, followed by the Hammersmith & City line in 1864, and the Bakerloo line in 1913. It is the first two that are of interest within the context of this book as for many years they were jointly owned and operated by the Great Western Railway.

The Metropolitan Railway.

During 1853 the Great Western became an interested party in the opening of London's first underground railway. The North Metropolitan Railway Co had been incorporated in 1853 to construct a new railway which would connect Paddington, via a series of tunnels, to King's Cross. The GW soon showed quite an interest in the project and agreed to subscribe a considerable sum of money towards the construction of the line. During 1854 the Metropolitan Co (the 'North' was dropped) was reincorporated, to construct a mixed gauge line from Paddington yard into the City. Money was slow to materialise and it was not until 1859 that the million pounds needed to construct the line was raised. During the same year a decision was made to terminate the line at Farringdon Street. In November 1861 the GW's interest bore fruit when it agreed to operate the line and, with new condensing locomotives designed by Gooch, the Metropolitan Railway was finally opened for traffic between Bishop's Road, Paddington, and Farringdon Street on 10 January 1863. Services were extended through to Aldersgate in 1865, Liverpool Street in 1875 and Aldgate in 1876. Unfortunately, the two companies soon started to fall out over both the working and the financing of the line and, on 18 July 1863, the GW gave notice that from 30 September it would withdraw its trains. The Metropolitan counteracted by operating a service using borrowed engines and rolling stock. These were obviously in poor condition for, on 9 May 1864, a Great Eastern engine exploded at Bishop's Road, luckily with no fatalities. Eventually order was restored and the GW relented. Under a new agreement, signed by the two companies on 11 August 1868, the GW was allowed to operate up to 12 passenger and seven goods trains daily in each direction to the newly-opened depot at Smithfield. All the trains were to be under the control of the Metropolitan, whose services also had precedence over GW trains. The GW had started to operate a broad gauge through service between Windsor and Farringdon Street on 1 October 1863 which, apart from a short break due to the disagreement between the two companies, continued to operate until the broad gauge was removed on 15 March 1869.

The Metropolitan was effectively extended westwards with the opening of the Hammersmith & City Railway on Monday 13 June 1864.

The Hammersmith & City Railway

The Hammersmith & City Railway was incorporated on 22 July 1861 to construct a line from Hammersmith to Bishop's Road, where its trains could use the Metropolitan Railway's tracks to the City. From the outset the new company was, to all intents and purposes, just an offshoot of the GW and Metropolitan with directors of both com-

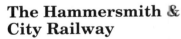

This early lithograph shows the entrance to the Metropolitan station at Bishop's Road c1864. Paddington station and the Great Western Hotel are seen on the right. *Great Western Trust*

panies on its board. The railway left the GW line at Green Lane Junction and ran for just over two miles before terminating at a small station near Hammersmith Broadway. The double track line was laid to mixed gauge to enable both GWR and Metropolitan trains to use the railway. Intermediate stations were situated at Notting Hill and Shepherd's Bush. The line was extended on 1 July 1864 with the opening of a ½-mile branch from Latimer Road Junction to connect with the West London Railway at Uxbridge Road Junction. Broad gauge passenger services, which were operated by the GW, commenced between Hammersmith and Farringdon Street on 13 June 1864 but, from 1 April 1865, this service was taken over by the Metropolitan Railway. The GW continued to run broad gauge trains through to Farringdon but these

Top:
A view dated around the turn of the century shows the entrance to the Great Western & Metropolitan station at Hammersmith. *Lens of Sutton*

Above
The Hammersmith & City station and bridge at Notting Hill and Ladbroke Grove on 9 September 1904. The entrance to the station is on the left at the foot of the bridge. *Lens of Sutton*

Right:
The exhibition station at Wood Lane was opened by the Great Western on the Hammersmith & City line on 1 May 1908. For such a permanent looking structure it was rather surprisingly closed on 1 November 1914. It was reopened on 23 November 1947 as White City but, again this was short-lived, the station being closed on 25 October 1959. *British Rail*

'Metro' class 2-4-0T No 3588 stands at Paddington Suburban (Bishop's Road) station with an up Great Western suburban service c1937. Although members of this class were fitted with condensing apparatus for working over the Metropolitan lines, No 3588 was not. *Great Western Trust*

ran via Latimer Road Junction and Kensington. In June 1865 management of the Hammersmith & City was placed in the hands of a joint GW and Metropolitan committee and, as a result, the GW agreed to lay an extra two tracks between Bishop's Road and Westbourne Park especially for Hammersmith & City trains. A new station was opened for Hammersmith & City trains at Westbourne Park on 1 February 1866. On 1 July 1867 ownership of the Hammersmith & City line was transferred to the GW and Metropolitan. During August 1868 the broad gauge was removed between Latimer Road Junction and Hammersmith and, on 15 March 1869, broad gauge services to Moorgate ceased. Interestingly, because of a delay in obtaining new stock, standard gauge services did not commence until 1 June 1869. General improvements to the line around this time saw a new station opened at Hammersmith on 1 December 1868 and at Royal Oak on 30 October 1871. The improved facilities at Hammersmith included a coal yard, engine shed and turntable. The engine shed was closed in 1905 but the coal yard here remained open until 1960. The GW also opened a small goods depot at Shepherd's Bush

Above:
Hammersmith & City line electric arrives at Platform No 13 at Paddington with a service from Whitechapel to Hammersmith. Notice the early colour-light signals on the right controlling Platforms Nos 11 and 12. *Great Western Trust*

Left:
This high-level view of the approaches to Paddington shows a Whitechapel-Hammersmith service pulling into Royal Oak station on 16 May 1973. *Brian Morrison*

on 29 July 1901. This depot remained open for coal and general goods traffic until 1 November 1967.

The general increase in traffic saw the junction at Westbourne Park become increasingly congested and, on 12 May 1878, a new tunnel junction was opened here to allow Hammersmith & City trains to pass unhindered under the main GW lines.

The two companies did not just operate train services. On 5 July 1875 Metropolitan and GW horse buses commenced running between Shepherd's

The terminus at Hammersmith today. Three platforms are still in use, notice also the GW-style roof canopies. Taken on 29 January 1993. *Author*

On 5 November 1906 the first of the new electric trains were introduced, but the whole service between Hammersmith, Addison Road and the City was not fully electrified until 1 January 1907. Power for the line was supplied from the new power station at Park Royal, which had been specially built by the GW for this purpose. The new electric trains were suitably inscribed 'Great Western and Metropolitan Railways'. New stations were opened at Wood Lane on 1 May 1908 (renamed White City on 23 November 1947), and at Shepherd's Bush on 1 April 1914 (this latter station replaced the original station here). During 1912 the tunnel junction at Westbourne Park was lengthened to allow for the expansion of the GW lines. At the same time the station at Royal Oak was reduced to just a single island platform. In 1933 the London Passenger Transport Act saw the Metropolitan Co replaced by the newly formed London Passenger Transport Board who, together with the GW, continued to operate the Hammersmith & City up until nationalisation. The GW's own City service was withdrawn on 16 September 1939. Today, the Metropolitan and the Hammersmith & City lines are operated by London Underground Ltd.

As both lines were initially worked by the GW I have included the following notes regarding motive power.

The first Metropolitan and Hammersmith services were hauled by 22 engines of the 'Metropolitan' class'. These 2-4-0WTs were designed by Gooch and constructed between 1862 and 1864. They were the first locomotives in the country to be fitted with condensing apparatus and the only broad gauge engines built for the GWR to have outside cylinders. They were not very successful and were replaced in 1866 with 0-6-0Ts of the 'Sir Watkin' class. These were probably the last broad gauge engines to work over the Metropolitan and Hammersmith branches. Narrow gauge services were operated up until electrification by members of the 'Metropolitan' class 2-4-0T and the '517' class 0-4-2T fitted with condensing apparatus. During 1933 11 members of the '57xx' class 0-6-0PTs, Nos 9700-10, were specially constructed with condensing apparatus for work over the Widened Lines to Smithfield.

Bush and Turnham Green. This service was short-lived, being replaced on 12 June 1876 by a new service from Hammersmith to Turnham Green. This also did not last long and, from 18 February 1878, was replaced by a service from Hammersmith to Barnes. This was obviously more successful and survived until 30 April 1899.

During 1882 a proposal was made to extend the H&C by constructing a new line from Latimer Road to the GW station at Acton. However, the project, like so many, suffered from lack of funds and was abandoned in 1900.

It is worth mentioning at this point that from c1894 and until electrification in 1906, the GW took over many of the workings of the Metropolitan Railway's service from Aldgate to Richmond via Bishop's Road, Grove Road Junction and Gunnersbury. Even after electrification the GW continued to operate a steam service from Notting Hill through to Richmond until December 1910.

The electric sheds at Hammersmith on 29 January 1993. Prior to electrification the Great Western had it own engine shed here. *Author*

6. The Branch Lines

The Brentford Branch

The use of the broad gauge by Brunel may have provided smooth travel for passengers but in terms of goods traffic it isolated the Great Western from other railways, particularly in London. Here the Great Western had no broad gauge access to any of the docks, which meant that coal and goods had to be transported across London from Paddington by road. To try and alleviate this problem the Great Western made available the sum of £25,000 to construct a new dock, canal wharfage, buildings and sidings at Bulls Bridge (Hayes) on the Grand Junction Canal. Bulls Bridge wharf was opened in the autumn of 1853, so goods and coal traffic could be transferred from the railway to barges here, and then taken along the canal to join the Thames at Brentford. In its first year of operation some 50,000 tons of coal were shipped this way. It must

have been a slow process for there were no less than 11 locks to negotiate over the six-mile journey. It was also an expensive way to move the coal for, apart from the cost of transferring it from rail to barge, there was also the canal toll to add to the cost.

It was because of these problems that, in 1854, a proposal was put forward by the Great Western & Brentford (Thames Junction) Railway to construct a broad gauge railway from the Great Western main line at Southall to the Thames at Town Mead, Brentford,

A pair of brand new Great Western diesel railcars Nos 19 and 21 stand alongside an unidentified '57xx' class 0-6-0PT at Brentford Town station on 18 June 1940. Being in such close proximity to the AEC works at Southall the branch was regularly used to run in the new railcars. *Ian Allan Library*

where a new dock would be built. Although independent the company was supported by the GWR with whom a provisional agreement was reached to work the line. There were obvious objections from both the canal company and the LSWR who had opened their own line to Brentford in 1853, but on 14 August 1855 the Great Western & Brentford Railway Act received Royal Assent. The canal company was appeased with a clause allowing them to work the new dock. The Great Western also agreed to close Bulls Bridge and to move the cranes and machinery to Brentford.

Interestingly the Brentford Branch was probably the last line to be engineered by Brunel and, as was usual, he had completely underestimated its cost.

Construction of the branch commenced on 3 March 1856 and owing to legal difficulties over some of the land, problems with subsidence at the dock

The small signalbox at Brentford Town station. The picture is undated but judging by the state of the box was taken sometime after it closed on 31 January 1954. *Lens of Sutton*

Passenger traffic was always sparse and even the introduction of steam railmotors on to the branch in 1904 and the opening of a small halt at Trumpers Crossing on 2 May of the same year failed to improve revenue. Passenger services were withdrawn, ostensibly as a World War 1 economy measure, on 22 March 1915 and probably would have have remained so, but local pressure saw them reinstated on 12 April 1920. Gradually, however, passenger services over the line declined. Trumpers Crossing Halte, the only intermediate station, was closed on 1 February 1926 and on 4 May 1942 passenger services were withdrawn from the branch — never to return.

The decline of passenger traffic was more than matched by an upturn in goods traffic. In September 1928 additional sidings were laid to serve the new Firestone tyre factory and the Imperial Biscuit Works (later Macfarlane Lang). On 3 November 1930 a new goods depot was opened at Brentford Town. Goods traffic over the branch continued to grow and by 1939 there were up to nine workings each weekday.

It was however the dock that provided much of the revenue for the line. It was situated at the point where the River Brent and the Grand Junction (later Union) canal joined the Thames. The whole complex was entered via a 29ft-wide tidal gateway. Initially much of the machinery at Brentford was steam-operated but, in 1919, the dock was extensively modernised by the Great Western and extended to cover an

enc and the need to raise extra capital, completion of the line fell behind schedule. It was eventually opened for goods traffic on 15 July 1859. Passenger traffic on the branch did not commence until 1 May 1860, the delay again being due to uncompleted work. The original intention was to build the terminus at the river's edge in order to connect with the ferry to Kew, but in order to save money this scheme was abandoned. Instead a small station was constructed at the western end of the town. Initially facilities comprised just a single platform and a wooden shelter but, in 1876 with the removal of the broad gauge, a second platform was constructed on the down side. Passenger services at this time comprised 10 or so services a day and, according to reports, were not very popular owing to inconsistent timing and the basic facilities provided at Brentford station.

The branch connected with the main line at Southall but did not run directly into the station. The original station here had been opened by the Great Western on 1 May 1839. Initially it comprised just two platforms but was extended in 1859 with the provision of a new bay for the branch services. In 1876 the station was extensively rebuilt to accommodate the new up and down relief lines.

The main priority of the branch was, of course, goods traffic and by 1861 some 66,000 tons of goods and minerals were being carried over the line annually. It had always been the intention of

the GW&BR to double the line and, during September 1861, this was done, in rather unusual fashion, with the laying of standard gauge track alongside the original broad gauge layout. The new formation, which was effectively a separate branch in itself, was opened on 1 October 1861 to coincide with the inauguration of standard gauge services between Reading and Paddington. In 1870 the line was finally taken over by the Great Western and in March 1876 the broad gauge line was converted to standard gauge.

The most important engineering feature of the line was (and still is) the Windmill Lane bridge. Here the road crosses over the canal and the railway passes under both, each at different angles. The canal itself is carried over the line in a cast-iron trough. This point became known as 'Three Bridges' and the total height from rail to road is about 35ft.

The only intermediate station on the Brentford branch was at Trumpers Crossing Halte which was opened on 2 May 1904. In this interesting picture the Southall-Brentford service is being worked by '517' class 0-4-2T No 833 which has been completely enclosed for auto working. Trumpers Crossing Halte (for Osterley Park) was closed on 1 February 1926. *Ian Allan Library*

The branch was originally constructed to serve Brentford Docks. The following four pictures show the dock in the 1930s.

This first picture shows the main river wharf and the two fixed cranes. On the right is one of the large warehouses. *Great Western Trust*

area of 15 acres. A new 900ft wharf was opened, increasing the wharfage at Brentford to 3,194ft. The dock itself was able to deal with craft of up to 300 tons. A feature that was retained was a large wooden shipping shed that had been designed by Brunel, but this was unfortunately burnt down in June 1920. It was replaced during the same year by a new steel and iron open-ended shed. The six warehouses were all equipped with hydraulic cranes and lifts and provided some 70,000sq ft of storage space. The large goods yard held nearly 1,000 wagons. In 1932 the docks were once again modernised with the provision of a pair of Cowans & Sheldon three-ton electric travelling cranes. Three electric capstans capable of moving 12 20-ton trucks were installed on the wharf. The dock became increasingly busy, dealing with such items as coal, timber, grain, scrap iron, general goods and motor vehicles. One of the sheds at Brentford Dock was used exclusively by Morris Motors and Nuffield Exports for the shipment of Morris Cars.

Returns for the year ending November 1956 show some 127,766 tons of general merchandise and 9,612 tons of minerals forwarded from Brentford docks with 52,288 tons of merchandise, 6,360 tons of coal and coke and 4,600 tons of minerals being received. Returns for Brentford Town goods were 30,769 tons of general merchandise and 167,772 tons of coal and coke arrived by rail. Rather surprisingly, during 1952 single line working was introduced over the branch. On 31 January 1954 the small signalbox at Brentford Town was closed and on 18 December 1955 the line between Southall and the Firestone siding signalbox was singled. Firestone Signalbox was itself closed on 30 May 1965.

The 1960s brought the Beeching cuts with the inevitable switch of goods from rail to road and, on 31 December 1964, Brentford Dock was closed. This was due, in part, to the cost of renewing worn out plant and also the poor road

Centre left:
The interior of one of the inner wharf warehouses. *Great Western Trust*

Left:
The special tipping bay used for loading coke from wagons into barges. *Great Western Trust*

Ex-Great Western 0-6-0PT No 9722 crosses the bridge at Brentford Dock with a permanent way train on 6 May 1962. *Leslie Sandler*

Below:
A feature of the branch are the three bridges near Southall where the road passes over the canal which in turn passes over the railway. Here on 21 April 1963 0-6-0PT No 9661 passes under the bridges on a Great Western Society special to Brentford. *R. N. Joanes*

Bottom:
The Brentford branch joined the main line at Southall and here, in the summer of 1950, '57xx' class 0-6-0PT No 5755 leaves the branch with some coal empties.The picture is also of interest as it shows the water softening plant (centre) and the old steam rail motor shed (left). *C. R. L. Coles*

access to the site. The track from the Tower yard to the dock was taken up during June 1965. However, the massive girder bridge over the Great West Road at Brentford was not removed until March 1976. Today much of the dock site has been converted to housing and the lock itself into a marina.

During May 1976 the Greater London Council signed a long-term contract for the conveyance of compacted town refuse. This is loaded at the Brentford refuse transfer station, which is situated on the site of the old town goods depot, and is conveyed in special container wagons to a tip at Appleford near Didcot. Currently there are six trips a week.

The old yard also contains a stone and limestone terminal operated by Messrs Day & Sons and is served as required by services running from Croft Quarry in Leicestershire.

At Southall the Associated Equipment Company (AEC) works was connected to the Brentford branch just south of the engine shed. For a number of years the works operated its own four-wheel diesel-mechanical locomotive. It is pictured here at Southall in February 1976. The AEC works closed on 25 May 1979. *Kevin Lane*

For a number of years Day & Sons have operated a limestone and granite terminal at Brentford Town Yard. The company operates its own locomotive, former BR No 12049 built at Derby in 1948, which is seen here at Brentford in 1984. *Kevin Lane*

Class 56 No 56039 runs on to the Brentford branch at Southall with rubbish empties from Appleford (Oxon) to the Brentford waste transfer terminal on 4 February 1990. The castle-like building in the background is an old water tower, built around the turn of the century and recently converted into flats. *Brian Morrison*

The Uxbridge Vine Street Branch

The short branch from West Drayton to Uxbridge Vine Street was actually the very first branch line to be constructed by the Great Western Railway in London.

For many years prior to the arrival of the railway Uxbridge was an important staging point for coaches on the Oxford-London road. The town, which lay about 15 miles from London, was actually quite important in its own right, with its own breweries, a corn-mill and a market. It was also served by the Grand Junction Canal, which had been opened through the town in 1798. The first mention of a railway at Uxbridge came in 1829 with an unsuccessful proposal to take the London & Birmingham Railway through the town. Certainly, at this time, the inhabitants of Uxbridge were generally anti-railway. However, the construction of the GW main line through West Drayton now brought a railway to within 2½ miles of the town and it was not long before the inhabitants of Uxbridge wanted their own railway.

On 16 July 1846 the Great Western & Uxbridge Railway obtained powers to construct a 2½-mile branch into the town from the GW main line at West Drayton. Unfortunately, as with many other schemes, money was not forthcoming but on 22 July 1847, the GW obtained powers to take over the construction of the line. For whatever reason nothing was done until 1853 when the GW obtained a third Act to construct a 2 mile 51 chain broad gauge line from the GW main line at West Drayton to a new terminus at Uxbridge near the Vineyard.

Construction of the line was relatively straightforward. Leaving the main line at West Drayton station it climbed up a 1 in 116 gradient to cross the Grand Junction Canal and the Cowley-West Drayton road. From here it passed to the east of the village of Cowley before terminating at Uxbridge Vine Street. The line was opened for passenger traffic on 8 September 1856. The terminus station at Vine Street was constructed of timber with an overall roof. It contained two tracks which served three platform faces. A fourth, and shorter platform was used as a loading dock. A goods shed, together with a small yard, stood on the west side. Other facilities here also included a small single-road engine shed and turntable.

Opening services comprised about 15 arrivals and departures each weekday and about 10 on Sundays. Records show that the engine *Vulcan*, built by Charles Tayleur at Newton-le-Willows and delivered to the Great Western in November 1837 which was converted to a 2-2-2T in 1846, hauled some of the first services over the branch.

During the weekend of 7/8 October 1871 the broad gauge was removed from the Uxbridge branch and standard gauge services commenced on the 9th. These would have almost certainly been in the hands of '517' class 0-4-2Ts. At this time the timetable contained several through services to and from Paddington and in 1879 services were extended to run, via Bishop's Road and the Metropolitan Railway, through to Liverpool Street. These services remained a feature of the timetable right up to the outbreak of war in September 1939. For a time there were also through services to Victoria, via Victoria Curve and Kensington. In 1880 the general increase in traffic saw the line doubled and on 2 October 1904 an intermediate station was opened at Cowley (about 1½ miles north of West Drayton). The station here comprised two platforms with the main offices on the up side. The small engine shed at Uxbridge was closed in December 1897 after which locomotives were serviced at Southall. The turntable was removed during 1899. It was probably at this time that a new 26-lever signalbox was

erected. This was situated on the west side of the line and in the station yard.

Services over the branch continued to grow, and in 1910 there were no less than 30 branch trains each weekday in each direction with a further 14 running through to the city.

During the 1930s a certain amount of rationalisation saw two of the platforms at Uxbridge removed together with the overall roof, and the resulting island platform was then covered with a standard type platform canopy. The through services to Liverpool Street were withdrawn during December 1939.

During the ensuing years the branch saw little change but in September 1958

Above:
This general view shows the island platform and the various goods sidings at Vine Street. *Lens of Sutton*

Right:
The only intermediate station on the line was at Cowley pictured here on 4 May 1960 as railcar No W30 awaits to depart for Uxbridge. The station was opened on 2 October 1904 and was closed on 10 September 1962 after which the line was singled. *A. A. Delicata*

Below right:
A pair of ex-Great Western diesel railcars Nos W24 and W25 approach Cowley on 4 May 1960 with the 9.15am service from Uxbridge Vine Street to West Drayton. *A. A. Delicata*

steam-hauled passenger services were replaced by DMUs and, from 27 July 1962, services were reduced to run at peak times only. Dwindling traffic and a certain Beeching report signed the line's death warrant, and on Saturday 8 September 1962 passenger services were withdrawn. The branch was singled on 18 October 1962 and on the same date the small signalbox at Uxbridge was closed. The line continued to be used by goods traffic until 24 February 1964 when the yard at Uxbridge was closed. On 2 July 1966 a new siding was brought into use about half a mile from West Drayton to serve the Middlesex Oil & Chemical Works. Services to the depot ran as required but did not last for long and on 8 January 1979 the last remaining portion of the Uxbridge branch was closed.

Railcar No W21 arrives at Uxbridge on 24 June 1960 with a service from West Drayton. In the background an 0-6-0PT shunts the daily goods. *A. A. Delicata*

The line was closed to passenger traffic on 10 September 1962 but remained open for goods traffic until 24 September 1964. Here on the last day of passenger services a DMU awaits departure for West Drayton and Yiewsley. A motor parcels van (later Class 128) stands at platform 2. *C. R. L. Coles*

Denham-Uxbridge

Rather surprisingly the Great Western opened a second branch to Uxbridge on 1 May 1907. The new branch, which initially was double track throughout, left the Acton-High Wycombe line via a triangular junction at Denham and ran for just 1¾ miles to terminate at Uxbridge High Street. Here a small single platform station was provided. This was mostly constructed of wood and stood above the town on a large embankment. The original intention of the GWR was to connect the Vine Street line with Denham on the Acton & Wycombe Railway and thereby form a through route, via the Metropolitan Railway, for services to and from the City. But, actually, to make the connection south of what was to become the eventual terminus at High Street would have required a considerable amount of extra engineering work. This included another large embankment and a steel girder bridge (which was actually constructed) to take the line over the High Street and, although a start was made on parts of this section, the GW decided that the potential traffic did not warrant the expense and abandoned the idea.

From the start, passenger services were operated using steam railmotors with up to nine services daily running in each direction between Uxbridge, Denham and West Ealing. These were extended at peak times and on Sundays with some services running through to Willesden Junction and some to Kensington Addison Road.

Uxbridge High Street is pictured here shortly after closure. Notice how the station was built on the side of the embankment, and also the footbridge and walkway from the High Street itself. *P. J. Garland/Courtesy Wild Swan Publishing*

Goods services were introduced on the branch from 11 May 1914 with the opening of a small low level coal yard to the west of High Street station, but as a World War 1 economy measure passenger services were withdrawn from the branch on 31 December 1916. These were not reinstated until 1 May 1919. The east curve at Denham East Junction, which was little used, was lifted during 1917 and, at the same time, the

branch was singled. Just prior to World War 2 passenger services were in the hands of '517' 0-4-2Ts and the newly-introduced '48xx' class 0-4-2Ts with nine services daily now running through, via Denham, to Gerrards Cross. Services over the branch never really came up to expectations and, from 1 September 1939, they were withdrawn for good by the GWR. However, the goods yard remained open and during World War 2 part of the old east curve at Denham was reinstated in

This second shot shows the general layout at High Street. The line terminated just beyond the platform. *P. J. Garland/Courtesy Wild Swan Publishing*

order to serve the nearby Anglo-American Oil terminal; the new siding came into use on 14 May 1942. After the war, goods traffic continued although, by the early 1950s this comprised just one daily service from Southall. On 28 October 1956 the high level platform tracks were taken out and a new run round loop was installed to serve the remaining coal sidings. Gradually, however, even this traffic declined and, on 24 February 1964, the Uxbridge branch was closed, although the short section from Denham West Junction to the nearby oil depot remained open until 7 November 1965.

Right.
An ex-Great Western diesel railcar traverses the Uxbridge High Street branch with a London Railway Society special in September 1954. *C. R. L. Coles*

Below.
Ex-Great Western 0-6-0PT No 3750 shunts the 5.25am goods service to Denham at Uxbridge High Street on 19 April 1958. Although the line closed to passenger traffic on 1 September 1939, the small yard here remained open for goods traffic until 24 February 1964. *Hugh Davies*

The Staines Branch

With the growth of railways in the 19th century many small towns sought to be connected to the network. Staines was no exception. In 1838, when the Great Western was opening the first section of its main line to Bristol, Staines was only a small market town situated at an important crossing of the Thames. Its first railway link came with the opening of the Windsor, Staines & South Western Railway (worked by the LSWR) on 22 August 1848. The arrival of the railway brought a certain amount of prosperity to the town and it was not long before the business interests cast their eyes northwards to the nearby GW. One early proposal, which did not get off the ground, envisaged a line from Acton to Staines and Egham. Another scheme to link Staines with the GW main line was made in 1866 with a proposal for single standard gauge line from West Drayton to connect with the LSWR line at Staines Moor, with part of the agreement being that the GW would work the line. A direct connection with the Uxbridge branch at West Drayton would allow through running between Staines and Uxbridge. However, as with many other schemes around this time, money was not forthcoming and the plan was abandoned.

In 1873 yet another proposal was put forward, only this time without the connection to Uxbridge and, on 7 July 1873, The Staines & West Drayton Railway Act received Royal Assent. Unfortunately, because of financial problems, nothing was done within the five year time limit. The Act was extended on 17 June 1878 and again on 11 August 1881. This latter Act included the reinstatement of the Uxbridge connection and a junction with the GW to the northwest of West Drayton station from where the line would pass under the GW main line. Again an agreement was signed by the GW that it would both work and maintain the line. The GW did not, however, like the idea of running on to LSWR territory at Staines, claiming that the LSWR station was poorly positioned and that its use would cause delays. The LSWR themselves were also lukewarm to the idea of GW trains running over its metals. The

Above right:
Yeoveney Halt looking towards Staines. The photograph is undated but shows the new curve connection (centre) which was opened on 23 June 1940 to connect the branch to the LSWR line at Staines Moor. The curve was closed on 15 October 1947. *Lens of Sutton*

Right:
Poyle Estate Halt comprised a standard concrete platform and open awning type shelter. It was opened on 1 April 1954 and served the adjacent trading estate. *Lens of Sutton*

problem was solved with a Bill that received Royal Assent on 2 August 1883 which allowed the GW to build its own separate terminus station at Staines.

The first section of the line, between West Drayton and Colnbrook, was opened on Saturday 9 August 1884 with a service of six trains per day. The financial troubles that had dogged the construction of the line for so long were still apparent when, in order to save money the contractor suggested that a private house near the site of the proposed terminus at Pound Mill in Moor Lane should be purchased and converted into the station building. The house in question belonged to one Charles Waring Finch, co-owner of Finch & Rickmans Mustard Mill, who traded in the town. The opening was delayed even further when, on 5 August 1885 a small bridge that carried the line over a stream collapsed. Eventually everything was finished and the 6¼-mile line was opened throughout on 2 November 1885, almost three years to

Ex-Great Western diesel railcar No W21 is seen here shortly after passing under the Great Western main line (left) at West Drayton with the 12.15pm service to Staines on 19 July 1958. *A. A. Delicata*

the day after work was first started. Passenger and goods receipts were initially disappointing. Records show that receipts for the first year of operation totalled just £1,075 11s 11d. Even the construction of a siding into the Linoleum works at Staines in May 1887 did not greatly improve matters. Linoleum had been invented in the town in around 1860 by Frederick Walton who constructed a factory to produce the material at Staines.

The terminus station at Staines provided by the company contained just one platform, a loading dock and a small goods shed and yard. Opening services comprised nine trains each week day to and from West Drayton where they shared the same island platform as the Uxbridge services. Staines branch passenger services were generally hauled at this time by the diminutive '517' class 0-4-2Ts. On 1 July 1900 the old S&WDR company was finally taken over by the GW.

Initially the only intermediate station on the branch was at Colnbrook. Here there was a passing loop and a small goods yard. Colnbrook was always

A single-car diesel-unit (later Class 121) on a service to West Drayton stands at the single platform at Staines West on 16 April 1960. *Hugh Davies*

West Drayton & Yiewsley Station.

The branch joined the main line at West Drayton. This picture was probably taken around the turn of the century from the up relief platform. The branch bay line is situated on the left. Interestingly the station sign reads 'West Drayton and Yiewsley Junc, for Uxbridge and Staines branches'. *Lens of Sutton*

a particularly busy station. In 1957, for example, it was dealing with 15,000 passengers and 30,000 tons of freight per year. A halt was opened at Runemede Range on 1 April 1887 (renamed Yeoveney from 4 November 1935). The platform at Runemede was actually only 20ft long, and was constructed to serve the nearby rifle range of the Metropolitan Rifle Range Co. It was apparently renamed by the GW because passengers were alighting here thinking they were at the Runnymede of Magna Carta fame, which was actually some six miles away. Other halts were opened at Stanwell Moor & Poyle on 1 June 1927 (renamed Poyle Halt on 26 September 1927) and at Poyle Estate on 1 April 1954, these latter two halts being actually only 65ch apart. The last halt to be opened on the line was Colnbrook Estate Halt which opened on 1 May 1961. The station at Staines was renamed Staines West on 26 September 1949.

On 23 June 1940 a new curve was opened at Staines Moor, just to the south of Yeoveney Halt, which gave a direct connection from the branch to the LSWR Staines-Windsor line and to Feltham Yard. The new curve saw frequent use during World War 2 as a diversionary route for freight trains. During the 1950s ex- GW diesel railcars were introduced on to some of the services and in June 1952 the small engine shed was closed and its allocation transferred to Southall. On 20 October 1953 goods services were withdrawn between Colnbrook and Staines West. One might be forgiven for thinking that this was a prelude to a general rundown of the line, but this was not the case. On 5 October 1958 steam traction, which was at this time in the hands of '48xx' class 0-4-2Ts, was withdrawn from passenger services and replaced by the newly introduced Diesel Multiple-Units. Services at this time comprised 18 each way on weekdays and 16 on Sundays. Gradually, however, passenger traffic declined. Sunday services were withdrawn in September 1961 and on 14 May 1962 Yeoveney Halt was closed. Passenger services on the branch were finally withdrawn on 27 March 1965. The branch was then used for a while as a testing ground for a new type of automatic train control but it seems that this did not last for long.

On 24 June 1964 a new terminal for domestic fuel oil was opened by Shell Mex & BP in the old goods yard at Staines West, being supplied at peak times by services from Ripple Lane. During the first months of operation this service was steam-hauled over the branch. In 1981 the construction of the new M25 saw the line south of Colnbrook closed and the oil terminal at Staines served via a new connection from the ex LSWR line. This came into use on 27 January 1981 and on the same date Staines West became part of the Southern Region.

Staines West oil terminal was finally closed on 24 June 1991.

Today the branch terminates at Colnbrook, where the station site is now covered by a Murco oil terminal which supplies aviation fuel to the nearby Heathrow Airport. In May 1984 Leicester's Bardon Hill quarry were awarded a £1.5 million grant to set up a stone terminal at Thorney Mill.

On 27 July 1981 a new connection was opened from Staines West Oil Terminal to the ex-LSWR main line. The new connection is seen here on the left as Class 37 No 37705 shunts tanks after arriving with the 10.10 service from Ripple Lane on 24 December 1990. The oil terminal at Staines was closed on 24 June 1991. *Paul D. Shannon*

The Windsor Branch

During the early days of railway construction one of the biggest problems for any company was the long list of protesters against the building of lines. The inhabitants of Windsor appear to have been somewhat different for they opposed the 1833 Great Western Bill 'because the railway did not run as near to the town as they would have wished'.

The construction of a branch to Windsor had been on the GW's mind for many years. Although the public of Windsor were generally in favour of the railway, progress was always stopped by the intransigence of the Provost and Masters of Eton College. It was these very same people who opposed both the 1833 Bill saying 'No public good whatever could possibly come from such an undertaking', and the 1835 Act insisting, in all they were overruled by the Lord Chancellor in June 1838, that the GW should neither stop their trains nor build any station within 3 miles of the college'.

A station was eventually opened at Slough on 4 June 1840. It was one of Brunel's one-sided stations and was constructed of wood and stood on the town (south) side of the line. Brunel's design contained what were essentially two separate stations — one for up trains and the other for down, but standing side by side on the same stretch of track. The advantages of this type of design were that passengers did not have to cross the lines and that non-stop trains ran clear of the station.

It was not until 1848 that the GW finally obtained an Act for the construction of a 3 mile 5 chain broad gauge forked branch 'from two points on the Great Western Railway near the western station at Slough' to Windsor. This time the Act was passed with the backing of the college but only after such

provisions as the planting of trees to ensure privacy for the bathing place, the provision of a clear waterway under the Thames Bridge, and an agreement that officials from the college should have free access to the station in order to apprehend any scholar who they considered should not be there. In fact, for a number of years, the GW was forced by the college to employ two special constables at Windsor solely for this purpose.

Work on the line started almost immediately, the only major engineering work being a 2,000yd long timber viaduct and a 213ft long single-span girder bridge over the Thames. Work progressed well and, on 8 October 1849, the line was opened for passenger traffic.

The original station at Windsor was of wooden construction, and its two platforms were covered by a large overall roof. The adjacent goods and carriage sidings were connected via a series of wagon turntables. There were no locomotive servicing facilities at Windsor so locomotives for the branch used the facilities at Slough.

Between 1861 and 1865 the old timber viaduct was removed and replaced by a new brick viaduct. This viaduct, which is still in use today, is 2,035yd long and contains some 300 arches. It was widened during the doubling of the branch in 1889. An interesting early feature of the branch was a special signal, designed by Brunel, called the 'Windsor Drum'. This had been introduced at Windsor, where the right-angle curve at the approach to the station rendered the ordinary disc and

An artist's impression of the original station at Windsor. Notice the mixed gauge track. *Great Western Trust Collection*

crossbar signal useless. In the horizontal or danger position there was a crossbar; in the vertical or 'All Right' position the driver saw first an upright bar and, as he rounded the bend, the usual disc.

The branch itself would have been rather nondescript but for the fact that, from its opening, it was used to convey Royalty to and from Windsor Castle. Queen Victoria had made her first journey on the GW from Paddington to Slough on 13 June 1842 and her first journey through to Windsor was made within a few days of the branch opening. The Queen obviously enjoyed travelling by train and had quite a say over the way the service was run. In 1898 the GW received the following telegram from Windsor Castle: 'Sir John McNeill (the Queen's equerry) says Her Majesty cannot understand why an hour and ten minutes should be allowed for her journey from Windsor Castle to Buckingham Palace, whereas it formerly occupied one hour. Sir John does not wish to explain to the Queen that longer time is taken by Her Majesty getting into and out of her carriage at each end. To avoid explaining this, he wishes the timetable supplied in the Queen's train to be shown as leaving Windsor at 11.25am, reaching Paddington at 12.00 noon. Actually Sir John wishes the royal train to be run from Windsor to Paddington in 30 minutes, and to leave Windsor as soon as her Majesty has taken her seat'.

At Slough the western fork of the branch became known as the 'Queen's Curve' because it was used almost exclusively by the Royal Train.

The branch was converted to mixed gauge on 1 March 1862. MacDermot states that, during this time, mixed gauge passenger trains were run over the branch, 'broad and narrow gauge vehicles being joined by means of a dummy coach'. Gradually, however, many of the services went over to the

The booking hall and platform entrance at Windsor is seen c1930. *Great Western Trust Collection*

standard gauge and, by July 1877, broad gauge services on the branch amounted to just two a day. On 30 June 1883 the branch was converted to standard gauge and in 1889 it was doubled throughout. The old single-sided station at Slough was replaced during 1886 with the structure that we can see today. The new station was provided with two main and two relief line platforms as well as two down bays, one especially for Windsor line services. Designed by J. E. Danks, it was built in the French style with three ornate pavilions, linked by low gabled roofs. No mention of Slough would be complete without mentioning 'Jim' the station's famous collecting dog. 'Jim' was presented to the railway in c1889 and commenced collecting at Slough when he was about four months old. He was taught to bark on receiving a coin and was also trained to do tricks. One of these apparently entailed him sitting in

a chair with a pipe in his mouth and a cap on his head! He could also stand on his hind legs. Over the years Jim collected about £100. 'Jim' died in 1896 and was afterwards placed in a glass case on the platform at Slough.

In June 1889 the Royal Agricultural Society held its Jubilee Show at Windsor which resulted in 246 special trains bringing in excess of 100,000 visitors.

Between 1895 and 1897 the old Brunel station at Windsor was extensively rebuilt. The new station was constructed in brick with moulded timbers and ornamental stone. It now contained four main platforms and a bay which were partially covered with a glass roof.

Part of the work included the removal of the old goods sidings, which were replaced by a new low level yard, and the construction of a new Royal station. This was constructed by the GW as a Diamond Jubilee gift to the Queen and was separated from the public platforms by a new carriage road over which was placed a large pediment bearing the date 1897. The Royal side of the station was covered by a large overall roof. One of the outstanding features of the 'Royal' station was the elaborately decorated waiting room. This was constructed of Bath stone and situated between the arrival platform and the roadway in order to allow carriages to

Although not of the highest quality, this picture is included as it shows Great Western diesel railcar No 1 leaving Windsor & Eton in June 1936 with a service to Slough. *Great Western Trust*

draw up under the glazed roof. The waiting room was used for arrivals rather more than departures, for, as soon as the train entered the branch, a telegraph message would be flashed from Slough to warn the officials to proceed to the platform in order to receive either the Monarch or her guests. The new facilities were first used by the Queen on 21 June 1897. Rather sadly Queen Victoria's last journey by rail was made on 2 February 1901 when a coffin containing her remains was conveyed in a specially-draped saloon from Paddington to Windsor on the occasion of her State funeral. In 1902, and in

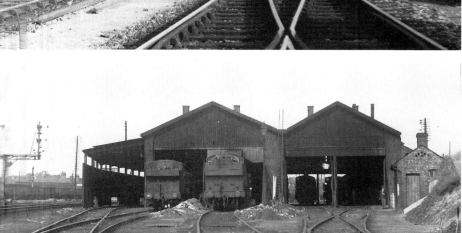

Above left:
Great Western Class '61xx' 2-6-2T No 6111 passes Slough West Junction and signalbox with a down stopping service to Oxford in c1946. *Lens of Sutton*

Left:
Motive power for the Windsor branch services was supplied from the small locoshed at Slough, pictured here in the early 1950s. *Lens of Sutton*

Below:
This general view of Windsor & Eton Central was taken in February 1962 and shows the station more or less intact with DMUs in two of the four platform lines. Windsor was renamed Windsor & Eton on 1 June 1904 and Windsor & Eton Central on 26 September 1949. *Photomatic*

anticipation of the Coronation of Edward VII and Queen Alexandra, the Royal rooms at the station were enlarged to provide a double suite.

Due to increasing subsidence, the Brunel girder bridge over the Thames was rebuilt in 1908. The original girder structure was found to be in quite good condition so the bulk of the work was centred on the replacement of the brick abutments.

The branch never saw a great deal of goods traffic but on 14 June 1912 a new siding was put in to serve the works of the Slough & Datchet Electric Light Co.

The only intermediate station on the line, Chalvey Road Halt, was opened on 6 May 1929. The GW had also proposed halts at Bath Road and Dorney Road but these were never built. It is interesting to note that even at this time Eton College complained that they had not been consulted over the opening of Chalvey. Whether or not this had any influence on the GW is difficult to say, for the halt was short-lived and closed

on 7 July 1930, after which the platforms and shelters were removed for reuse at Cashes Green Halt in the Stroud Valley. By the 1930s the line was very busy with 37 trains daily in each direction, some of which ran through from Paddington. The Sunday service which comprised 28 trains each way was very popular with tourists. During 1950 the station was renamed Windsor & Eton Central. On 27 January 1952 the only industrial siding on the branch at Chalvey was closed.

The 1960s saw the closure of many of the Thames Valley branches but, apart from Henley, Windsor was the only other London suburban branch that did not feature in the Beeching axe. In order to keep the line open, a certain amount of rationalisation took place. On 9 September 1963 the line was singled with control of the branch passing to the newly opened panel box at Slough. Goods services were withdrawn from the branch on 6 January 1964, and the low level yard was removed in April of the same year. In August 1966 the

Windsor Borough Council approved a plan by BR and Railway Sites Ltd to close the station at Windsor and to construct a new terminus a quarter of a mile west. The old site would have then been redeveloped to provide a shopping centre, hotel and bus station but, luckily, the scheme was abandoned. Further rationalisation took place when, on 17 November 1968, Platforms Nos 3 and 4 were closed and, on 5 October 1969, the station was reduced to a single platform with the closure of Platform No 2. The remaining platform was itself shortened on 22 November 1981. By this time the station was generally in a poor state and in 1982 a joint effort between BR and Madame Tussaud's saw the refurbishment of the Royal side of the station, which is a Grade Two listed building, to form the basis for a 'Royalty and Empire' exhibition. The royal suite of rooms, which were last used for royal purposes during the funeral of King George V on 28 January 1936, were completely refurbished back to their original state. The station itself had been used for King George VI's funeral train on 13 February 1952 but, by this time, the royal rooms, which had previously been used for general storage, had been converted into the divisional headquarters of the railway police. The police eventually moved out and prior to restoration the rooms were in use as a newsagent's shop. The main entrance, together with the trainshed roof, were also refurbished and in the platform was placed a replica of a Dean 'Single' No 3041 *The Queen* together with two royal coaches — one an original and the other a replica. During 1991 Madame Tussaud's sold their interest in the exhibition and, although still open, the future use of the old Royal station looks uncertain.

Windsor today is served by half hourly services from Slough, which up until the start of the 1993 summer service were still being operated using 30-year old 'heritage' DMUs. Loadings, however, are good so the future of this once royal branch seems secure.

As a footnote, the Headmaster of Eton College has still, in theory, got the power to search the station and trains for errant Etonians.

Left:
Class 121 No 55031 and trailer No 56283 forming the 19.41 service from Windsor is pictured here as it aproaches Slough on 30 July 1981. *Les Bertram*

Below:
Class 121 unit No 55024 and trailer No 56283, forming the 14.11 service from Windsor, run off the branch at Slough on 18 September 1982. *Michael J. Collins*

The Wycombe and Marlow Branches

One of the more unusual of the surviving Thames Valley branch lines is that from Maidenhead to Marlow. This is because it was originally constructed as two separate railways: the Wycombe Railway from Maidenhead to Wycombe and the Great Marlow Railway from Bourne End to Marlow.

The Wycombe Railway company was incorporated by an Act of Parliament on 27 July 1846 to construct a branch from Maidenhead to High Wycombe. Like many similar schemes at this time money was a problem and the powers lapsed. However, the scheme was revived by an Act in 1852. Work was started during the same year but was not completed until July 1854. After the usual inspection the line was opened for passenger traffic on 1 August 1854. The new branch, which was leased to the Great Western at a fixed rent, left the GW line at 'Wycombe Junction', about 1½ miles west of the original Maidenhead station and approximately on the site of the present station. MacDermot describes the branch as 'a single line of cheap construction, not quite ten miles long, laid with Barlow rails weighing 90½lbs to the yard and 12 inches wide at the bottom'.

There were five intermediate stations — at Maidenhead Wycombe Branch (from c1866 this station was known as Maidenhead Boyne Hill), Cookham, Marlow Road, Wooburn Green and Loudwater. The station at Maidenhead was situated adjacent to the Bath Road at Castle Hill. It was closed on 1 November 1871 when the present station at Maidenhead was opened.

At Bourne End there were two timber viaducts: one over the Thames and the other over the water meadows at Cock Marsh. It was this latter viaduct that had caused the delay in construction of the line. The viaduct here was eventually replaced by an earth embankment. The first station at High Wycombe was constructed of wood and had a single platform with an overall roof. A small engine shed stood adjacent to the station. The coal stage and turntable were, however, some distance away. The first services over the line were hauled by a pair of 'Wolf' class

Above right:
The Wycombe Railway station at Marlow Road seen in 1869. Notice the early type signal at the road crossing. Marlow Road was renamed Bourne End on 1 January 1874. *Great Western Trust*

Right:
This lovely old shot shows Marlow station c1883. The engine is a '517' class 0-4-2ST No 522 which was altered to a pannier tank in February 1884. *Great Western Trust*

broad gauge engines, *Aurora* and *Javelin*.

Wycombe station was rebuilt when the branch was extended through to Princes Risborough and Thame on 1 August 1862. The line was extended from Princes Risborough to Aylesbury on 1 October 1863 and from Thame to Oxford on 24 October 1864. The whole section from Maidenhead through to Oxford was converted from broad to standard gauge between 23 August and 1 September 1870 and, on the same date, the engine shed at Wycombe was closed.

The first idea of a railway from Marlow Road (Bourne End) to Great Marlow was discussed by the directors of the Wycombe Railway Co at their board meeting on 9 November 1854. However, it appears that public opinion was not on their side and the proposal was quietly dropped.

In 1864 the Wycombe Railway, together with the GWR, resurrected the idea, proposing extensions of its lines to both Uxbridge and Marlow. After much wrangling over the distribution of receipts and opposition from local landowners the Bill was withdrawn on 23 February 1865. After yet another

false start the businessmen of Marlow decided to go it alone and, in August 1867, the Great Marlow Railway Co was formed. The Wycombe Railway had been absorbed by the GW on 1 February 1867. The Great Marlow Railway Act, to construct a 2m 60ch single line from Marlow Road to Great Marlow gained Royal Assent on 13 June 1868. However, recurring financial problems saw the start delayed and it was not until September 1872 that an agreement was reached with the GW to construct the line jointly.

Construction of the branch finally started in March 1873 and, with no major engineering work, was finished by 17 June. The official inspection took place on 25 June and, since there were no obvious problems the inspector, Col Yolland, pronounced that 'the line may be opened at once'.

On 28 June 1873 the Great Marlow Railway was officially opened for passenger traffic, just in time for the Marlow Regatta. The first train left Marlow at 8.30am and was, according to the local paper, 'liberally patronised'.

To avoid confusion the station at Marlow Road was renamed Bourne End on 1 January 1874. The station at Great

Marlow was constructed of brick and contained a single platform. A small engine shed was provided for the branch engine, and a goods shed stood in the yard opposite. At Marlow Road the branch ran into a bay platform built along the back of the existing single platform. Train services initially comprised 10 each way daily with four on Sundays. The line was a great success and, by 1876, passenger figures had risen to over 87,500 a year. In 1897 the Great Marlow Railway was finally taken over by the GW and on 23 July of the same year the GWR promoted the Marlow & Henley Railway to link the two branches, but this scheme never materialised.

The rather crude arrangements at Bourne End continued until 1894 when the GW undertook improvements to the station. These included the provision of an up platform, a new double junction to give direct access to the branch and a new branch platform complete with run round loop. The new up platform was linked to the downside by a new footbridge. The whole station complex was also resignalled, being controlled by two new signalboxes at Bourne End North and Bourne End South.

In 1895 the old wooden viaduct across the Thames at Bourne End was replaced by a new steel and cast-iron girder structure. It seems that the old viaduct, which had already been extensively repaired in 1873, had been in quite a dangerous state for some time.

In January 1914 a new type of electric train staff was introduced between Bourne End and Marlow. On the new system, the instrument was simplified and the old staff was replaced by a key or 'token'.

Little change took place on the line until the 1930s when the town of Maidenhead was expanded northwards and on 5 July 1937 the GW opened a new halt on the old Wycombe Railway section, 1½ miles north of the junction at Maidenhead. It was originally intended to call the halt 'North Town Halt' but, instead, it was opened as Furze Platt Halt. The station at Maidenhead was a particularly busy place, figures for 1960 show that it was dealing with 303,000 passengers and 15,000 season tickets each year as well as 110,000 parcels and 83,000 tons of goods.

On Sunday 8 July 1962 steam services were withdrawn from the branch, and were replaced by a single car diesel unit. For many years the steam service to Marlow had been hauled by '48xx' 0-4-2Ts and was known locally as the 'Marlow Donkey'. Goods services to Marlow were withdrawn on 18 July 1966 and on 10 July 1967 the old station at Marlow was closed. Passenger services were switched to a new 80yd long platform that had been erected in the old goods yard. Goods services to Bourne End, which for many years included wood pulp and coal for the nearby paper works, were withdrawn on 11 September 1967. During 1968 ser-

vices between Maidenhead and Aylesbury were rationalised and the intermediate stations at Wooburn Green and Loudwater were reduced to unstaffed halts (goods services were withdrawn from these stations on 18 July 1966).

On 5 May 1969 the through services to Aylesbury were withdrawn leaving only a limited service between Maidenhead and High Wycombe. Passenger numbers over this section plummeted and on 4 May 1970 the five-mile section of the old Wycombe Railway between Bourne End and High Wycombe was closed. The last service had actually run two days before on Saturday 2 May.

The writing appeared to be on the wall for the Maidenhead-Marlow section but, in February 1972, the Marlow Railway Passenger Association was formed to persuade the Western Region to keep the branch open. Such was the success of the Association that, during the 1970s, a considerable sum of money was spent by the Western Region in modernising the branch. The work included the refurbishment of the remaining stations and complete resignalling of the branch, which then came under the control of Slough. Today the branch is as busy as ever with 20 services a day in either direction between Marlow and Maidenhead. There is, however, no Sunday service. At Bourne End the Marlow branch platform has now gone, the siding area being occupied by industrial units. Marlow services now use the old down platform where reversal takes place. At Marlow only basic facilities are now provided, and the single platform contains only a bus-type shelter.

The '517s' were replaced on Marlow trains with '48xx' class 0-4-2Ts and these types continued to operate the bulk of the branch passenger services up until the end of steam, although many were renumbered in the '14xx' series. Here No 1421 waits at Marlow on 17 February 1962 with the 12.20 pm through service to Maidenhead. *Leslie Sandler*

'48xx' class 0-4-2T No 1450 being coaled on the shed siding at Marlow in 1958. This small single-road shed was closed in July 1962. *J. D. Edwards*

Above:
A single diesel-unit in green livery arrives at Furze Platt Halt in the early 1960s with a Maidenhead-High Wycombe service. *Ian Allan Library*

Left:
Class 121 unit No 55024 departs from Loudwater with the 16.00 service from High Wycombe to Bourne End on 21 June 1969. This section of the line was closed on 4 May 1970. *J. Vaughan.*

A through service from Paddington to High Wycombe approaches Bourne End on 5 September 1959 hauled by ex-Great Western 0-6-0PT No 3697. *C. R. L. Coles*

Facing page top:
Class 61xx 2-6-2T No 6117 leaves Furze Platt Halt on 7 July 1962 with the 4.15pm service from Maidenhead to High Wycombe. *Leslie Sandler*

Facing page bottom:
Ex-Great Western 0-4-2T No 1421 stands at Bourne End on 7 July 1962 with the 2.29pm service from Marlow to Maidenhead. *Leslie Sandler*

Right:
Another 0-4-2T, No 1445, takes water at Maidenhead prior to working the 2.14pm service to Marlow on 1 July 1962. It appears that the fireman has something in his eye. *Leslie Sandler*

An up goods hauled by 0-6-0PT No 5766 runs through Bourne End on 17 February 1962. *Leslie Sandler*

The old Wycombe branch now terminates at Bourne End. Here on 27 May 1981 single cars Nos W56281 and W55023 wait to form the 13.13 service to Marlow. *Brian Morrison*

The Henley on Thames Branch

There were various plans for a railway to Henley, the earliest being the Tring, Reading & Basingstoke plan of 1833. A further three proposals were made in 1845 by the South Midland & Southampton Railway, the Midland Grand Junction and the Great Western, all of which were unsuccessful. Although the other proposals fell by the wayside, the Great Western tried again the following year and on 22 July 1847 obtained authority to construct a 4½-mile branch from the main line at Twyford. Unfortunately, at this time, the GW was having difficulty financing the project and, although the line was surveyed and marked out, the scheme was shelved. It was obviously the GW's intention to construct the line at some stage, for, in 1852, they obtained an extension of time on the 1847 Act. By this time the inhabitants of Henley were getting restless at the lack of action by the railway. After representations by the Mayor and many important businessmen in the town the GW finally resolved to construct the line, provided the people of Henley contributed one-third of the estimated £45,000 cost. This was soon agreed, although various deviations from the proposed route were suggested. However, the GW decided to construct the line as surveyed and on 4 August 1853 the revived 1847 Act received Royal Assent.

In February 1854 the GW invited tenders 'for the construction of the Henley Branch Railway, a length of about 4½ miles'. The branch would be built as a single-track broad gauge line with provision for possible doubling in the future. Work was started around January 1855 and progressed slowly. At Twyford the branch ran through the old goods yard, effectively dividing it in two. Its construction also required the removal of the brick goods shed that had been constructed in 1845. Twyford station itself had been rebuilt in 1846 using brick and stone, and up and down platforms were staggered. In 1857 the up platform was extended into the goods yard to provide a new bay platform for Henley branch services. At the same time a new footbridge was

Above right:
The driver of '517' class 0-4-2T No 463, c1910, seems to be eyeing up these rather eloquent lady passengers at Shiplake — one of the two intermediate stations on the branch. *Great Western Trust*

Right:
A general view of Shiplake around the turn of the century. Notice the interesting track in the small yard. *Lens of Sutton*

installed, connecting up and down platforms.

Leaving Twyford the branch crossed the Thames at Wargrave and the Lashbrook at Shiplake, both on timber viaducts. A small intermediate station was provided at Shiplake. The attractive station provided at Henley was constructed of brick with a wooden overall roof. Although, no early plans of the station exist, it appears that it was provided from the start with three platforms. A small single-road engine shed and a 45ft turntable stood in the yard alongside On 25 May 1857 the finished line was inspected by Col Yolland, the Board of Trade Inspector, who declared it satisfactory.

Top:
The second station on the branch was at Wargrave, pictured here in the 1930s. *Lens of Sutton*

Above:
Henley in BR days with '94xx' class 0-6-0PT No 9403 waiting to depart with an afternoon service to Twyford and Reading. At this time the station still had three platforms. *Lens of Sutton*

On Monday 1 June 1857 the new branch was opened for passenger traffic. The event was celebrated by a public breakfast at Henley town hall, after which the first train left for Twyford, at approximately 8am, hauled by the locomotive *Virgo*, a 'Leo' class 2-4-0T. There were five services daily in each direction with four on Sundays.

The branch, of course, was particularly busy during the Royal Regatta week with many extra services being run, many right through from Paddington. Regattas at Henley had been established in c1839 but it was not until 1851, when Prince Albert became patron of the Regatta, that the term 'Royal' was used. Right up until the present time around 20,000 extra passengers are carried over the branch during Regatta Week.

The 10.00am local goods service from Henley on Thames to Reading, hauled by ex-Great Western 0-6-0 No 2248, approaches Twyford on 22 April 1964. By this date this was the only goods service over the branch. *B. K. Snow*

Single-car Class 121 No W55030 waits
under the overall roof at Henley with
the 13.06 service to Twyford on 21 June
1969. *John Vaughan*

structed on the south of the old formation. The new station, constructed by
Jackaman & Sons, now contained four
main platforms and a branch bay. The
new lines were opened for traffic on
4 June 1893.

The gradual increase in traffic to
Henley was causing the operating
department problems. It had always
been the GW's intention to double the
branch, and at a company board meeting on 23 July 1896 the decision was
taken to undertake the work. The estimated cost of the doubling was put at
£21,275. As part of the work the old
wooden viaduct at Shiplake was
replaced by a new iron girder structure,
and a three-span brick arch viaduct was
constructed over the flood plains at
Wargrave. At Shiplake a new island
platform was provided. The whole line
was resignalled with new boxes being
constructed at Henley and Shiplake.
The doubling was finally completed on
11 July 1898. Interestingly in July
1897 the GW was considering a scheme
to extend the branch from Henley to
Marlow but after considerable local
opposition from the inhabitants of Henley the scheme was dropped.

By 1868 services over the branch had
increased to eight each way on weekdays and four on Sundays. From c1867
trains on the branch were controlled
using train staff and block telegraph,
and during the 1870s semaphore signalling was brought into use.

On Friday 24 March 1876 the branch
was converted from broad to standard
gauge, in record time it seems, for the
work was started by about 700 men at
9.30pm and was finished by 8am the
next morning. After conversion the little
'517' class 0-4-2Ts took over many of the
passenger services.

Over the years various improvements to the line took place. In 1881 the
main up platform at Henley was lengthened and in 1887 the second platform
was similarly treated. Henley had, by
now, become a busy station and, in
1895, the platforms were once again
lengthened and additional sidings were
put in.

With the end of the broad gauge on
the main line in May 1892 the GW
undertook the task of quadrupling the
line between Taplow and Didcot. This
necessitated the complete rebuilding of
Twyford station and the provision of a
new bay platform for Henley branch
services. The old main line was converted into the up and down relief, and
the two new main lines were con-

In this May 1977 view the old station
building has been demolished. Class 121
No 55030 departs with the 14.25 service
to Twyford. *Les Bertram*

The branch had now become very busy with many through services running to and from Paddington. On Monday 1 January 1900 a new intermediate station was opened at Wargrave. Unlike Shiplake, the station at Wargrave was provided with separate up and down platforms linked by a footbridge. During the same year a new direct non-stop service was introduced between Paddington and Henley, with a journey time of just 50min. Being near to the GW signal works at Reading, the branch was used during 1906 for testing an early form of ATC (automatic train control) equipment.

During 1914 a new steam railmotor service was introduced between Henley, Reading and Basingstoke. By this time services to and from Twyford were in the hands of 'Metro' class 2-4-0Ts, with Churchward 'County' class tanks and '36xx' class 2-4-2Ts operating the Paddington services. The provision of a 55ft turntable at Henley in 1903 allowed the use of larger engines such as 'Bulldogs', 'Dukes', and 'Counties' over the branch. During the 1930s the 'Metros' were replaced on the branch by '57xx' class 0-6-0PTs and the new Collett '48xx' 0-4-2Ts. In 1934 some of the new AEC diesel railcars were tried on the branch. Also, at this time, many of the through trains from Paddington were hauled by the larger Collett types such as 'Halls' and 'Castles' but, because of the small turntable at Henley, these had to be turned at Reading.

During the 1950s the branch was very busy. Figures for 1957 show that Henley was dealing with 65,000 passengers and 2,700 season tickets per annum, 9,000 parcels in and 30,000 out and a further 22,000 tons of coal, coke and agricultural traffic.

Very few additional changes took place until, on Sunday 5 October 1958, steam traction was withdrawn from the branch services. The regular '57xx' class 0-6-0PTs were replaced by one of the new single car diesel units. On the same date the small engine shed was closed. Steam haulage continued on the Paddington services until they too were officially withdrawn on Friday 14 June 1963. Under the Beeching cuts of the early 1960s, the Henley branch was one of the few in the London area that did not have to fight to remain open. How-

ever, a certain amount of rationalisation did take place. The branch was singled between 11 and 20 June 1961. This entailed the removal of the down running line. At Wargrave, facilities were provided on the up side only, the down platform being closed and removed, but at Shiplake the down line was retained as a passing loop. Colour light signals were installed on the branch together with a new signalbox at Shiplake (which was opened on 14 June). The decline continued, however, and from Monday 7 September 1964 goods services were withdrawn from the branch. For many years the daily goods service left Reading at 4.35am arriving at Henley at 7.00am. The return working left Henley for Reading at 9.00am. From the start of the 1968 timetable locomotive haulage was withdrawn from the Henley-Paddington services and replaced with redundant 'Inter City' type DMUs.

On 16 March 1969 the track into platform 1 at Henley was removed and on 11 May the loop at Shiplake was taken out. On 20 March 1972 signalling on the branch was transferred to the

new power box at Reading and the boxes at Henley and Twyford were closed. Through services between Henley and London were withdrawn from the end of the summer 1974 timetable.

During May 1975 the overall roof together with the station buildings at Henley were removed. Much of the adjacent land was sold or used for car parking. It was not until 1986 that a new station building was provided at Henley. At the same time the track layout was reduced to a single platform. During September 1985 the station buildings at both Wargrave and Shiplake were removed, and were replaced with basic shelters. During the summer of 1990 the girder bridge at Shiplake was extensively rebuilt, and for several weeks services over the branch were suspended.

Today there are 22 services each way daily between Twyford and Henley, which, from the start of the summer 1993 timetable, were operated using the new Thames Turbo Units, one of which forms a morning 'Regatta Express' through train to Paddington. There is currently no Sunday service.

7. Paddington

As mentioned in Chapter 3, it was Brunel's original intention to use the London & Birmingham station at Euston for his terminus. This was not to be, and on 3 July 1837 permission was granted for the Great Western to extend its line from Acton to Paddington. A large area of land at Paddington was purchased from the Bishop of London to construct the new terminus. Once again the GW directors were forced to change their plans. The company considered it essential to open the line as soon as possible and, with the delay in obtaining the Act for the final section into Paddington and the need to construct a new road bridge to take the Bishop's Road over the railway, there was no time to build a permanent station. Instead Brunel built a temporary station on the area to the west of the Bishop's Road bridge that had originally been earmarked for his goods depot. This was built two years later to the east of the bridge (on the site of the present station).

This first, temporary, station at Paddington (which actually lasted for 16 years) was constructed almost entirely of wood. In order to save money the entrance, booking office and waiting rooms were situated under several of the arches of the Bishop's Road bridge. Initially, the station was provided with a single island platform which served for both arrivals and departures but, in 1839-40, a second pair of platforms, for arrivals only, were constructed to the north of the station approach road. The new layout effectively divided the station into two, and the confined nature of the site also meant that each platform was a different size: departure Platform No 1 measured 240ft x 17½ft; departure Platform No 2 was 235ft x 17ft; arrival Platform No 1 was 255ft x 25ft; and, arrival Platform No 2 was 340ft x 34ft.

Many references suggest that the whole area of the platforms was covered over, but early plans of the station seem to indicate that this was not so and that only the departure side was covered. It is, however, possible that some sort of cover for the arrival side was erected later but, since the station was only designed as a temporary structure, perhaps the company did not want to spend any more money than was necessary.

A large engine house (described in detail in the chapter on Locomotive Depots) and a 180ft x 70ft carriage shed were also constructed in the yard. Entrance to the carriage shed was effected via a 22ft traverser, which also linked the various platform lines. A large wooden goods shed, 330ft long and 120ft wide, was constructed on land to the east of the Bishop's Road bridge.

Right:
Queen Victoria's funeral procession arrives at Paddington on 1 February 1901. This picture is particularly interesting as it shows the original buildings on the London Street side of the station. *Great Western Trust*

Looking in absolutely pristine condition 'Achilles' class 4-2-2 No 3029 *White Horse* stands at Paddington around the turn of the century. The engine, which was rebuilt as a 4-2-2 in July 1894, was withdrawn in May 1909. *Ian Allan Library*

As services developed it became quite obvious that a new station was needed at Paddington. In February 1851, and probably in anticipation of the opening of the extension through to Birmingham and South Wales, the directors agreed to build, to the east of the Bishop's Road Bridge, 'a passenger departure shed, with offices, platforms, etc, and proper approaches on the ground beyond the present goods shed. And to agree for building on the company's property an hotel with refreshment rooms, dormitories, stables and other conveniences adjoining the Paddington Station, and to procure the money, not exceeding £50,000, requisite for the purpose, either by lease or mortgage of the premises or upon the credit of their undertaking, and to let the premises on lease when built'. In 1852 a further £75,000 was made available for the purchase of additional land together with the construction of a goods warehouse, an engine house, additional sidings and offices. In order to construct the new station Brunel enlisted the help of his friend the architect Sir Matthew Digby Wyatt. The lack of room, caused partially by the continued use of the goods shed, saw construction of the new station (or half of it for as yet no mention seems to have been made by the GW regarding the arrival side of the station) fall behind schedule. This was obviously

DESCRIPTION.

1. Verandah in front of booking hall.
2. Booking hall.
3. Booking office.
4. Luggage way and auxiliary booking office.
5. Station master's office.
6. Waiting rooms, &c.
7. Down parcels office.
8. Carriage entrance.
9. Carriage exit.
10. Cloak room and lost property office.
11. Arrival exit.
12. Up parcels office.
13. Arrival waiting rooms.
14. Traversers between departure platform lines and adjoining sidings, by means of which trains could be strengthened or lightened without shunting. Probably used also for forming trains on departure lines, without recourse to locomotives.
15. Examination pit.
16. Overhead gangway, connecting with offices over carriage shed. Probably used for observation purposes by Traffic officers.
17. Carriage shed with offices over. In these offices were probably housed the Manager, Secretary, and other chief officers of the Company.
18. Steps giving access to offices.
19. Carriage sheds.
20. Traverser serving carriage shed.
21. Yardmen's shelter.
22. Shear legs. Probably used for lifting engines under repair. The turntable giving access to the siding under these shear legs is of much greater diameter than the one in the engine shed, and presumably, therefore, there were in existence about 1845 some engines which could not be turned in the engine shed.
23. Traverser used for goods traffic.
24. Goods sidings and platforms under bridge.
25. Carriage landing.
26. Police office.
27. Yard cranes.
28. Goods offices.
29. Traverser.

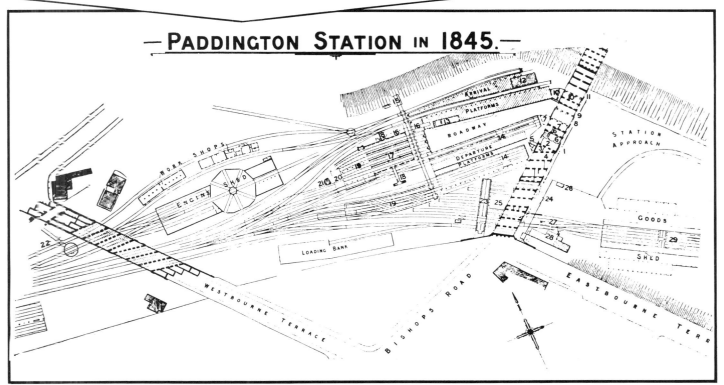

PADDINGTON STATION IN 1845.

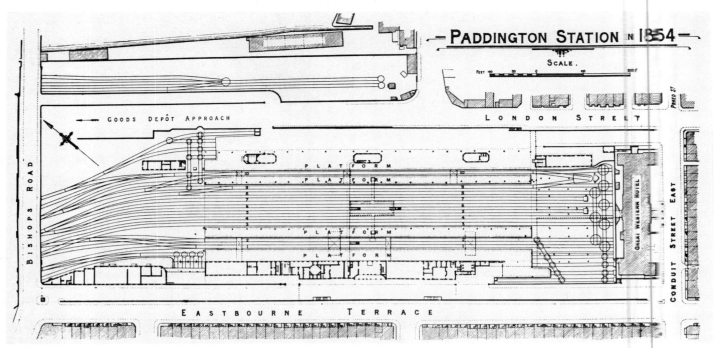

GOODS DEPÔT APPROACH

BISHOPS ROAD

PLATFORM

PLATFORM

PLATFORM

PLATFORM

EASTBOURNE TERRACE

LONDON STREET

GREAT WESTERN HOTEL

CONDUIT STREET EAST

SCALE.

an intolerable situation which was summed up by a report by Brunel to the Directors when he stated that 'the difficulties of proceeding successfully with different portions of new work on the site of old buildings, without interfering too much with the carrying on with traffic in a station, already far too small for the wants, have been very great'. In February 1853 the directors decided that the new arrival shed should be built forthwith and made a further £75,000 available to complete the project. Progress was obviously still slow as, in August, Brunel reported that 'the works at Paddington station for the passenger trains are still much in arrear, but are advancing towards completion. The alteration of the main lines, approaching Paddington, has been effected, and the engine house is in course of construction upon the site of the original line of the railway. As soon as it is completed, the old engine house may be removed and the extension of the goods department, so much needed, may be commenced'. The departure side of the new station was brought into use on 16 January 1854. At this time trains still terminated at the old station but, on 29 May 1854, the arrival platforms were at last opened for use and the old station at Bishop's Road was closed for good. The new station added about 20ch to the mileage from London. It was to take a further 18 months to finish the new station, construct the engine house, carriage shed and goods depot.

The Great Western Hotel was built in the style of Louis XVI and was actually the first of the great railway hotels. It was opened for business on 9 June 1854 when it was inspected by Prince Albert and the Prince of Wales.

The hotel was connected to the passenger station by a large footbridge,

which also connected the station to nearby London Street. The bridge appears to have been taken down in c1880.

The whole project at Paddington had cost a total of £650,000 and gave the GW one of the finest stations ever built.

A contemporary work about Brunel describes the station thus: 'the interior of the principal part of the station is 700ft long and 238ft wide, divided in its width by two rows of columns into three spans of 68, 102 and 68ft and is crossed at two points by transepts 50ft wide, which give space for very large traversing frames. The roof is very light, consisting of wrought iron arched ribs, covered partly with corrugated iron and partly with the Paxton glass roofing, which Mr Brunel here adopted to a considerable extent. The columns which carry the roof are very strongly bolted down to large masses of concrete, to enable them to resist sideways pressure. This station may be considered to hold its own in comparison with the gigantic structures since built, as well

A particularly interesting photograph which was taken from the end of Platform No 1 and shows the original Paddington Arrival signalbox. This box was closed and replaced by a new box on 19 April 1914. Arguably of greater interest is the large stone building in the centre. This was the station hostel, for guards, porters and other staff. It was opened in 1854 and stood at the end of the main arrival platform. It was demolished during station reconstruction work in May 1914. *Ian Allan Library*

as with older stations. The appearance of size it presents is due far more to the proportions of the design than to actual largeness of dimension. The spans of the roof give a very convenient subdivision for a large terminal station, dispensing with numerous supporting columns, and at the same time avoiding heavy and expensive trusses. The graceful forms of the Paddington station, the absence of incongruous ornament and useless buildings may be appealed to as

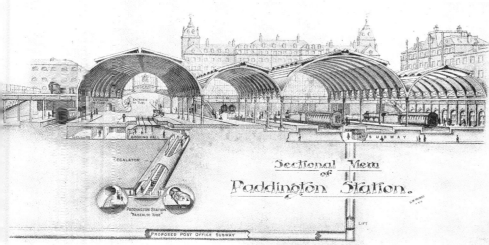

a striking instance of Mr Brunel's taste in architecture and of his practice of combining beauty of design with economy of construction'.

The platform layout of the new station was quite unusual. Within the train shed were 10 lines: three for departures, five for carriage storage and two for arrivals. On the arrival side there was a refreshment room, a cloakroom, a left luggage office, and various waiting rooms. At the western end of the main arrival platform the company constructed a large building which was occupied by guards, porters and other staff. (It was demolished during reconstruction work in 1915.) A series of turntables was provided at the Bishop's Road end of the station on both the arrival and departure sides. It appears that these were used for the loading of private carriages in which the owners were going to travel. All the turntables were removed by c1867. Reference to the 1854 plan shows a pair of 'auxiliary' island platforms with no obvious connection to either the main arrival or departure platforms. The connection was actually provided by five movable 'traversing' platforms — two on the departure side and three on the arrival side. This description of the movable platforms is taken from the 1876 publication *Railway Appliances* by John Wolfe Barry:

'At the Great Western station at Paddington, the booking offices are placed by the side of the main departure platform. A piece of cross platform, on a truck, is provided which when required is drawn out by hydraulic machinery from beneath the main departure platform, and rises to the same level as the main platforms, becoming a bridge across the rails, and giving access to the second departure platform.

This interesting photograph was taken during the locomotive trials in 1925 and shows LNER Class A3 Pacific No 4474 (here unnamed but later *Victor Wild*), arriving at Paddington on Tuesday 28 March with the up 'Cornish Riviera'. *P. J. Reed/Great Western Trust*

'By the use of this movable platform three long trains can be loaded at once, if the two trains nearest the booking offices be temporarily cut in half. When it is necessary to despatch these trains, the movable platform is run back to its position beneath the main platform, the first half of the train is backed and coupled up to the second half. Trains of shorter length can be loaded and despatched, when the movable platform is raised. The position of the booking offices, near the centre of the departure platform, is no doubt convenient, as the passengers approach the train near its centre: and though there is some inconvenience in the use of the movable platform, the arrangement answers well for a terminal station like Paddington where trains are not very frequent, while the central position of the booking offices is certainly advantageous where the amount of passengers' luggage is large.'

By 1892 four of the traversers had been removed, but that connecting Platforms Nos 1 and 2 remained in situ until c1920.

Some idea of the use of the new station can be gleaned from an 1854 census which shows that 1,400,000 passengers used the new station during its first year.

Paddington was actually the first station to be equipped on a large scale with hydraulic machinery. This was supplied by Armstrong Whitworth & Co for 'the loading and unloading of trucks, the hoisting into warehouses the lifting of loaded trucks from one level to another, the moving of turntables and the hauling of trucks and traversing machines'. Between the platform ends and the hotel, on the area known today as the 'Lawn', were various lines and turntables. Some of these were of 22ft diameter and were probably used for the loading and unloading of mail vans but, by about 1868, much of the track and turntables had been removed.

The origin of the 'Lawn' is unclear. The GWR magazine states that prior to the erection of the Great Western Hotel

Westbourne Terrace and the entrance to Paddington in 1922. The terrace contained many hotels. On the right is the small kiosk occupied at this time by Ernest Young who sold chocolate, fruit and flowers. The kiosk, which was originally constructed as a GWR enquiry bureau, was removed during the 1930s station rebuilding programme. *British Railways*

in 1854 the circulating area behind this building was verdure clad'. The area is also mentioned in a letter of complaint, to the *Times* newspaper, dated 24 May 1839, but because of the date must refer to the old station at Bishop's Road: 'At the entrance of the Great Western Railway at Paddington there is a grass slope, parted off merely by a post and rail, so that any person, by stooping may pluck the grass. There unfortunately happened to be a wallflower growing, and a young lady, about 10 years old, the daughter of a timber merchant in the Harrow Road, was tempted, unconscious of doing wrong, to take a sprig of about three inches long: she was immediately seized by one of the police and brought weeping before a tall man dressed in the costume of the Company, who in no very soft tone called "Lock her up; carry her away and lock her up" The terror and entreaties of the poor girl for mercy were heartrending, but of no avail, and she was separated from the servant and placed in confinement'. The young lady was apparently 'liberated' within a quarter hour but the letter also states that, on the same day, three other women were apprehended for the same reason. The company was, of course, heavily criticised for its action. In defence a company inspector stated that: notwithstanding notice boards

cautioning people not to trespass on the slopes, he found people constantly trampling them down and wantonly destroying the shrubs and flowers'. A further reference states that the area in question was actually the stationmaster's garden, so this might explain the rather over zealous reaction, but not unfortunately the exact location of the 'Lawn'.

In May 1861 mixed gauge tracks were laid between Reading and Paddington and on 14 August 1861 the first standard gauge train, albeit an engineering inspection train, arrived at Paddington. From 1 October of the same year standard gauge services commenced between Paddington and the West Midlands.

On 10 January 1863 the first section of the Metropolitan Railway, from Paddington Bishop's Road to Farringdon Street station, was opened for traffic. The station at Bishop's Road was constructed of timber with an overall roof. It had two platforms and was, for a time, the terminus of the Metropolitan

This picture, taken from the GW magazine, shows Whiteley's 'digital'-type clock being erected on the 'Lawn' at Paddington in March 1934. Some idea of the size of the clock can be seen by comparing the figures with the man on the ladder. *Great Western Trust*

A high-level view shows the entrance to Paddington in 1935. The extended suburban platforms can be seen on the upper left as can the newly-constructed Arrival signalbox. On the right are the offices of the parcel forwarding department. *Ian Allan Library*

Railway. On 13 June 1864 the Hammersmith & City Railway was opened between Bishop's Road and Hammersmith. This company was itself taken over by the GW and Metropolitan companies in July 1867.

With the increase in services, an additional arrival platform (today Platform No 9) was constructed at Paddington in June 1878. This required the repositioning of the cab road and the construction of a new overhead cab ramp. On 1 January 1881 electric lighting was used for the first time at the station. Initially power was provided by a small generating station situated at the eastern end of the Bishop's Road down platform and operated by the Brush Electric Light Co. This, apparently, proved to be unreliable and in, 1884, a contract was signed for a new plant. In April 1886 power generation was taken over by the Telegraph Construction & Maintenance Co using three generators designed by J. E. Gordon. Whereas the old system covered only part of the station, the new layout used up to 5,000 lamps and included all platforms and offices, the Hotel, goods station, yards and also Westbourne Park station. The *Electrician Magazine* for May 1886 states: 'The installation at Paddington is the first effort to be made in England to give a continuous supply of electric light on a very large scale, analogous to the rival illuminant, gas'. In 1887 the generating plant was taken over by the GWR. Subsequent rebuilding work at Paddington saw the power station closed and, from April 1907, power was supplied, via a new sub-station at Royal Oak, from the the GW's own plant at Park Royal. This had been built in 1906 to supply power for the newly-electrified Metropolitan and Hammersmith lines. Paddington was actually one of the first buildings in London to be illuminated by electricity. During the same year the station buildings on the departure side were extended and a new set of steps connecting the Hotel with the main departure platform was constructed. A new milk platform was also opened on the up side of the station, behind the main arrival platform. Although details are

sketchy, it was probably around this time that the remaining tracks and turntables were removed from the 'Lawn' area.

By 1884 the general layout at Paddington was as follows: Platforms Nos 1,2 and 3 were for departures; and, Platforms Nos 8 and 9 were for arrivals. Between Platforms Nos 3 and 8 were Nos 4, 5, 6 and 7 lines. These were used as sidings for stabling, cleaning and examining trains. Lines Nos 1, 2, 6 and 8 were available for both broad and narrow gauge trains; the rest were for narrow gauge only. There were three small turntables at the western end of Platforms Nos 8 and 9, and these were used for loading horseboxes and trucks.

Many of the employees at Paddington were evidently regular church-goers as apparently on Sundays, at this time,

the station doors were closed after the departure of the 10.40am train and were not reopened until after the church services were over, when the first Sunday afternoon train, the 1.45pm to Windsor, was due out. This custom seems to have been discontinued on 26 June 1903 and after this the station was open throughout the day.

On 28 February 1884 an attempt was made to blow-up the station by placing a bomb in the down cloakroom. The bomb, containing a timer device and 22lb of dynamite, was believed to be the work of the Fenian Brotherhood (a group of Irish sympathisers). It appears that similar devices had been placed in the cloakrooms at Charing Cross and Victoria and a decision was made by Mr W. A. Hart, the GW's London divisional superintendent, to search

This atmospheric shot was taken on a February morning in 1935. Notice how open the 'Lawn' area appears to be and also the footbridge on the left which connected the Hotel to the Lawn area. *C. R. L. Coles*

The magnificent roof provides a fine setting for the sad occasion of the funeral of King George V on 28 January 1936. The funeral train carrying the King's remains was hauled to Windsor by 'Castle' class No 4082 *Windsor Castle* (foreground). The coffin can just be seen alongside the train and below the platform No 8 sign. *Great Western Trust*

the luggage deposited in the cloakrooms at Paddington; it was he who found the bomb concealed in a small brown bag. The Home Office specialist who later defused the bomb came to the conclusion that it had failed to explode because the timing clock was placed upside down and had stopped! Sadly, some things never change, for, on 18 February 1991, an IRA bomb exploded between Platforms Nos 6 and 7 at Paddington, causing only minor damage but much disruption.

The opening of new carriage sidings at West London in 1885 allowed the remaining sidings at Paddington to be used for the construction of two additional departure platforms. These were opened during May and were constructed between Nos 4 and 5 storage sidings.

On 20 May 1892 broad gauge services came to an end, and the subsequent removal of the remaining track allowed yet another platform to be constructed. The work was completed during 1893 and now gave Paddington a total of nine platforms. These were incorporated without any expansion of the station itself and were numbered in sequence from the departure side outwards. During 1905 a parcels subway together with electric goods lifts was constructed to link Platforms Nos 1, 2, 3, 4 and 5.

For many years one of the most well known features at Paddington has been the large three-sided clock, which was installed in 1903 on Platform No 1. Each face measures 7ft 6in and the clock itself stands some 18ft above platform level. In 1929 its clockwork mechanism was removed and the clock was converted to the electric-pulse system controlled from a master clock situated in the stationmaster's office.

A particularly interesting feature of many GW stations at this time were the railway collecting dogs. The British public have always been great animal lovers and these dogs were very popular. Probably the most famous of all was Paddington's 'Tim'.

'Tim' operated at the station for about 12 years and in that time he collected over £1,000 for charity. In May 1900 he was, by special command, presented to Queen Victoria and in February 1901 he was similarly honoured by a presentation to King Edward VII. 'Tim' died in c1905 and, after a visit to the local taxidermist, his preserved remains were placed on display in a glass case on Platform No 1. In order to put what he collected into perspective

'King' class 4-6-0 No 6017 *King Edward IV* enters Paddington in the summer of 1936 with a service from Birkenhead. Notice the writing on the goods shed announcing 'one day transits between important towns'. *C. R. L. Coles*

new roof will replace the 'ridge and furrow' roofing' (this 'Paxton'-style roofing covered part of the arrival side roadway, Platform No 9 and the milk platform). 'The high level road running parallel will be supported on a "cut and cover" principle to enable the furthermost line to be laid below. No 9 platform will be extended to 950ft, and a new cab ramp will replace the present access to the carriage road a second ramp giving access to the carriage road of the new platform'. (By 1938 2,500 cabs each day were passing through the arrival side of Paddington.) The subway is to be extended to serve the new platforms and a footbridge will be built to

with today's values the amount should be multiplied by about 100.

By the turn of the century, passenger traffic had increased considerably and very soon the GW Board was looking at ways to enlarge and modernise Paddington. Plans for the work, which were approved in 1907, proposed a general updating of facilities: 'to extend the accommodation on the arrival side by the construction of three additional platform lines, each 800ft long, two for passengers and one for milk traffic. A second line will be laid beside the existing No 9 platform line; a platform (with carriage road occupying its centre) will intervene; and the two further lines beyond will be bounded by a milk platform adjoining Bishop's Road station: a retaining wall abutting Bishop's Road tunnel and extending thence to the other end of the station completing the work on this level'. (This wall which was 10ft thick and 15ft high, also supported the Grand Junction Canal Co's premises as far as South Wharf Road, a distance of some 550ft.) 'Overhead, a

Above right:
The entrance to Paddington at Westbourne Terrace after the air raid of 16/17 April 1941, when the area was hit by a parachute land mine. Apart from the damage shown, many of the terrace buildings here were severely damaged. *Great Western Trust*

Right:
Paddington actually got off quite lightly during the war as far as damage was concerned but arguably the worst incident occurred when the station suffered a direct hit by a pair of 500lb bombs on the evening of 21 March 1944. This picture taken on the morning after shows the extent of the damage. The rest of the station was apparently back in action during the same day. *Great Western Trust*

lead to Bishop's Road station, where also the platforms will be widened and lengthened.

In April 1907 a new stationery stores and printing works were opened at Paddington. The new building, which was situated adjacent to Royal Oak station, comprised four floors and a basement and measured 81ft long and 103ft deep. In later years this building was used as the Western Region historical records office.

Work on the station improvements was not started until 1909 and proved to be difficult because of the lack of space. In order to incorporate the new platforms, a considerable portion of the high-level coal yard was demolished along with part of the company's 'Mint' horse stables. Major engineering work entailed diverting London Street to run over the new platforms via a steel girder bridge for a distance of 189ft between Francis Street and South Wharf Road.

Platform No 12 was the first to be completed, on 10 November 1913, and measured 750ft x 35ft. It was used for the loading and unloading of general perishables such as milk and fish. The two new passenger platforms Nos 10, opened on 31 December 1915, and 11, opened on 10 May 1914, measured 800ft x 18ft and 830ft x 18ft respectively. Connection between these two platforms was via a scissors crossing. As already mentioned, the large staff building at the west end of Platform No 9 was demolished. Each of the new platforms were fitted with Ransomes & Rapier hydraulic buffer stops, the first of their type to be used on the GW. At the same time Platforms Nos 1, 2 and 3 were also extended. A 70ft x 33ft hydraulically-operated traverser table manufactured by Tannett, Walker & Co was fitted between Platforms Nos 9 and 10. The traverser had a capacity of 145 tons and was able to move 11ft 2½in in either direction at a speed of 20ft per second. An interesting feature of the traverser was that, when it was stationary, the structure rested on a set of traverse rails thereby removing the whole of its weight from its wheels. When an engine ran on to the traverser, eight small hydraulic rams would lift the table from its rest and place it back on to its wheels.

Probably the most interesting part of the work was the provision of a new train shed. This was constructed to match Brunel and Wyatt's original

The vehicular entrance on the arrival side at Paddington pictured here on 25 July 1946. Behind the retaining wall on the right is London Street. Notice also the company crest above the entrance. *Ian Allan Library*

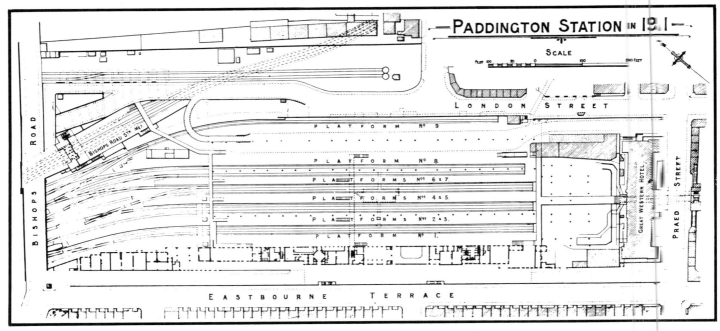

PADDINGTON STATION IN 1911

design of 1854. The main body of the work was undertaken by Jackaman & Son of Slough and Holliday & Greenwood Ltd of Battersea with the steelwork sub-contracted to Horseley & Co of Tipton.

The steel ribs of the roof of the new train shed were considerably stronger than the 1854 wrought-iron ribs. They measured 109ft across and were spaced at 10ft intervals along the 700ft length of the roof. Each rib weighed about four tons. The supporting columns were 2ft 4in wide, 24ft high and weighed 13ton. They required special 16ft square foundations in order to spread the load on the soft London clay. The roof covering consisted of some 40,000sq ft of Rendles 'Invincible' glass, interspersed with galvanised iron sheeting. The whole area of the new roof, which was finally completed during 1916, measured some 1¾ acres and increased the roof area at Paddington to 3½ acres. Other work carried out included the provision of large cellars under Platforms Nos 10 and 11. The cellars, which were opened on 25 July 1914, measured 500ft long and between 34 and 56ft wide. In later years further cellars were opened under both the Lawn area and Platform No 1.

Above left:
Yet another Royal Funeral: the scene at Paddington on 15 February 1952 on the occasion of the funeral of King George VI. It was for this occasion that the Western Region did the famous locomotive swap (No 7013 for No 4082 which was in the works at the time). Notice also the special seating that was installed over Platforms Nos 9 and 10.
Great Western Trust

Left:
The view of the roof of the train shed at Paddington pictured here in September 1951. *M. Earley*

'Castle' class No 4096 *Highclere Castle* stands at Platform No 9 on 24 March 1951, after arriving with the 8.20am service from Weston-Super-Mare. At Platform No 10 is 'King' No 6005 *King George II* with the 7.30am service from Shrewsbury. *Brian Morrison*

Brown Boveri gas turbine No 18000 heads out of Paddington and away to Old Oak in June 1952 with the empty stock of an up Bristol service. *P. Ransome-Wallis.*

Other alterations included the widening of the roadway, from 20 to 25ft, between the arrival platforms and Praed Street. Work was completed on 2 January 1915 and actually entailed removing part of the goods department and repositioning the station superintendent's office above the entrance. The new road surface into the station was laid using 'Durax' sett paving, which apparently provided a better foothold for horses in the wet. A new parcels distribution area was set up on the 'Lawn'.

The whole reconstruction project took nearly seven years to complete, although it must be said that some of this delay must be put down to the outbreak of World War 1.

On 1 December 1914 the Bakerloo extension line between Edgware Road and Paddington was opened for traffic. The new underground station was connected to the main line station above by moving escalators.

On Armistice Day in 1922 the GW war memorial to the 2,524 GW employees who lost their lives in World War 1

was unveiled at Paddington by the then Chairman of the company, Viscount Churchill. The memorial, which stands under the central transept on Platform No 1, is still in situ today, and is in the form of a bronze figure of a soldier. It was designed and sculptured by Capt C. S. Jagger with the surrounding architecture being designed by T. S. Tait. It was rededicated on Friday 11 November 1949 when Sir James Milne unveiled the additional tablets with the names of the 794 GW men and women who gave their lives during World War 2. The names of all of those who were killed are contained in a sealed lead container which was placed under the bronze figure.

During 1922 a start was made on the gradual replacement of the old cast-iron columns of Brunel's original roof with new steel hexagonal columns, after considerable wastage had been found in the 1854 structure. The work was undertaken by the Cleveland Bridge & Engineering Co of Darlington. In order to minimise disruption the work was

undertaken by replacing just one platform at a time and was not finally completed until 29 March 1924.

In order to take some of the pressure off the booking staff at Paddington a new central information bureau was opened adjacent to the station at 5 Craven Road in 1928. An article in the 1932 GW magazine states that the new bureau was dealing with over 50,000 enquiries a year. During 1923 the refreshment room on Platform No 1 was refurbished and the main dining room was enlarged. The refreshment facility was certainly busy as the following statistics of one day's business at this time shows: 3,800 cups of tea, 850 pots of tea, 4,300 cakes and buns, 2,750 sandwiches, 650 portions of bread and butter and 650 pieces of fruit.

Under the Government Loans and Guarantees Act of 1929, £1,000,000 was made available for the 'completion of improvements at Paddington'. The new work comprised the extension of main line platforms, and roof coverings, to give a minimum length of 1,000ft with a

Compared with Great Western engines I personally think the BR Standard classes, although impressive looking, lacked that certain *je ne sais quoi*. Fellow Great Western enthusiasts will known what I mean. It is illustrated here in this 1952 shot of 'Britannia' Pacific No 70020 *Mercury* as it awaits departure from Paddington with the 6.55pm service to Swansea.
Brian Morrison

maximum of 1,240ft along with remodelling of the permanent way at the western end. An extensive scheme of development of the 'Lawn' and the construction of two blocks of offices. The provision of a new parcels depot and the enlargement of the Bishop's Road station. Other important work included the complete remodelling of the trackwork on the approaches to Paddington for a distance of ¾ mile and the provision of power-operated points and colour-light signalling. Work was started during May 1930 and was finished in the autumn of 1934. The signalling scheme provided three new power-operated signalboxes: Westbourne Bridge (into use 10 January 1932); Paddington Departure (into use 2 July 1933); and Paddington Arrival (into use 13 August 1933). The first two were direct replace-

Ex-Great Western 2-6-2T No 6163, on station pilot duty 2, waits to take the stock of an up Worcester train back to Old Oak Sidings for servicing on 6 April 1963. *Derek Tuck*

ments for the old mechanical boxes but the new Arrival box replaced the old Arrival, Bishop's Road and Royal Oak boxes. Incidentally, the new box at Westbourne Bridge was the first on the GW to have an all-electric interlocking frame. As already mentioned the track was remodelled out as far as Ranelagh Bridge and all unnecessary pointwork was removed from the platform roads.

During the summer of 1933 Bishop's Road station was demolished and replaced by a new station with four platforms each 600ft long. The construction of the new platforms at Bishop's Road also entailed the removal of part of the shed at Paddington goods and the demolition and subsequent reposition-

ing of some of the offices. At the eastern end of Bishop's Road some 30ft of rail tunnel was removed to allow the area to be widened. The new station, which was opened on 18 September 1933, was designated Paddington Suburban, its platforms being numbered 13, 14, 15 and 16. Platforms Nos 13 and 15 were served by Hammersmith & City electric services and Nos 14 and 15 by GW suburban services. A ¼-mile long parcels subway was constructed to connect the new platforms at Bishop's Road to the new parcels depot and also to the old subway under Platform No 1. The new parcels depot was opened in 1952 and was served by an extension to Platform No 1. The new platform was designated

Smoke and steam as 'Castle' class No 5022 Earl of Eldon departs from Paddington with the 'Cambrian Coast Express': the 10.10am service to Aberystwyth and Pwllheli. *Peter Treloar*

parcels Platform 'A' and 'A South'. The new parcels platform and the main departure platform were essentially one platform 2,660ft long. For many years the GW and the Western Region stabled restaurant cars alongside Platform No 1A for battery charging and servicing Platforms Nos 2-11 were either expanded or refurbished to give an additional 2,200ft of platform length. At the western end of the station a new

footbridge, which also carried a booking office, was constructed to connect all the existing platforms with the rebuilt Bishop's Road station.

Two new steel-framed office blocks were constructed on either side of the 'Lawn'. On the arrival side the office was built in the contemporary style. It was 118ft long and had eight floors and a partial basement. The walls were lined in black Victoria stone and were set on a plinth of polished granite. Outside, the building was adorned with the words 'GWR Paddington 1932'. Then, on the departure side, the new offices were constructed to match Brunel's original design. The refurbished station together with goods and parcels depots, now cov-

ered an area of 72 acres. The construction of the new parcels depot had allowed the 'Lawn', which for many years had been the centre of parcels operations at Paddington, to be cleared to form a concourse fit for, in the GW's own words: 'The Gateway to the West'.

An interesting feature of the remodelled 'Lawn' area was the provision of a large electrically-operated 'digital'-type clock. The clock was designed and man-

The 'Mayflower' headboard being fitted to 'Warship' class No D842 at Paddington on 14 April 1961. Notice the 83D (Plymouth Laira) steam type shed plate on the front bufferbeam.
B. R. Tunnard

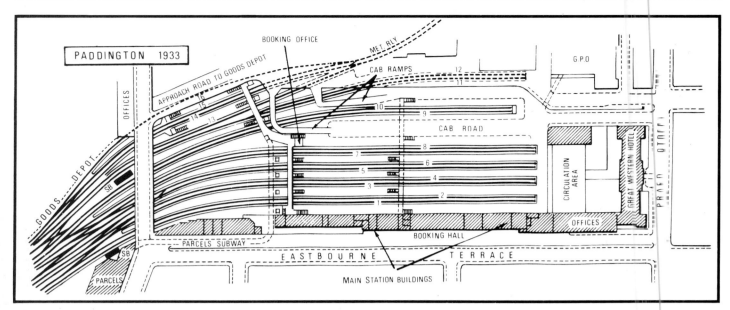

PADDINGTON 1933

APPROACH ROAD TO GOODS DEPOT

BOOKING OFFICE

MET. RLY.

CAB RAMPS

G.P.O.

OFFICES

GOODS DEPOT

SB

CAB ROAD

CIRCULATION AREA

GREAT WESTERN HOTEL

PRAED STREET

OFFICES

PARCELS SUBWAY

SB

PARCELS

EASTBOURNE TERRACE

BOOKING HALL

MAIN STATION BUILDINGS

ufactured by Gillett & Johnson Ltd of Croydon and installed by William Whiteley Ltd of Queens Road, London. It was said, at the time, that the clock was the largest in the world. Its figures were over 3ft high and moved on a roller blind system, each movement taking about eight seconds. In order to improve information for the travelling public a large electrically-operated train indicator, the first of its kind in the world, was installed in the centre of the 'Lawn'. The indicator was manufactured

'Hymek' No D7023 arrives at Paddington in September 1962 with the 6.45am 'South Wales Pullman' service from Swansea. At this time a 'Blue Pullman' set was working this service but had obviously failed, hence the substitution with locomotive and coaches.
B. Haresnape

by the Siemens & General Electric Railway Signal Co Ltd and was brought into use on 27 March 1934. It replaced a smaller indicator that was situated on Platform No 8. The new indicator consisted of a polished teak frame with eight panels facing in the arrival direction. Each of these showed the arrival time of a particular train together with the platform number, minutes late, stations served, etc. Departure information was displayed in the same way but on the reverse of the indicator. The whole indicator was controlled from a small panel room situated on Platform No 1. Another interesting feature of the station at this time was an electric bell, fixed to a cross girder above the roadway and near the Platform No 8 subway. The bell was operated from the arrival box and was to inform the porters, via a series of codes, at which platform the next train would arrive.

On 22 May 1935 a fully-equipped Crown Post Office was opened at the entrance to Platform No 1 by the Postmaster General, Sir Kingsley Wood. The Post Office was the first to be opened on a railway station in this country. During 1936 amplified train announcements were introduced at Paddington. It appears that the vast roof initially caused problems with the acoustics and that over 40 loudspeakers placed at 30yd intervals were needed to cover the platform areas alone. Announcements were made from a small office that stood on the covered bridge over the 'Lawn'. Work on the station was not finished until 1938 with the reglazing of the No 1 bay roof.

World War 2 saw Paddington become a busy place, first with the evacuation from London of many thousands of civilians, and throughout the war by the movement of service personnel. In 1940

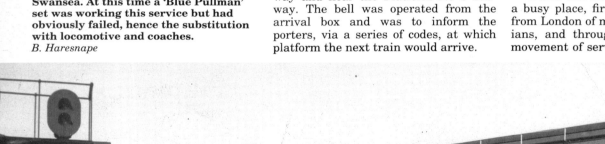

the staff dining room, which had been opened in August 1939, was converted to a Forces canteen. During the same year the underground cellar stores under Platforms Nos 10 and 11 were converted into air raid shelters. During the war they were also in use as a crèche for children up to the age of 14.

As with many other stations Paddington suffered damage during World War 2. The station and approach lines were hit on several occasions. Paddington Goods depot was hit by high explosive bombs on 24 September 1940, 12 November 1940 and 11 May 1941, and again on 14 March 1944 by a Phosphorous incendiary bomb.

On 17 April 1941 a parachute landmine landed near the Eastbourne Terrace entrance, causing considerable damage to the offices on the departure side and the adjacent terrace houses. On 11 May 1941 Platforms Nos 12 and 13 were damaged by a 500lb high explosive bomb. The station was hit three times on the evening of 22 March 1944 when a pair of 500lb bombs came

through the roof, one of which landed near the London Street entrance and failed to explode, the other exploded on Platforms Nos 8 and 9 causing a 12ft deep crater and destroying about 50ft of platform. The third was a Phosphorous incendiary bomb. This landed adjacent to the 'Lawn' area and, fortunately, did little damage. Paddington Goods yard and depot was also hit on four occasions. Over the duration of the war the station itself was hit just seven times; two of which, it must be said, were by our own 'stray' anti-aircraft shells! Finally, to explode a myth (excuse the pun) the station was never hit by a V1 flying bomb.

On 11 December 1943 an interesting ceremony took place at the station when

the first of the American loan locomotives, 'S160' 2-8-0 No 1604, was officially handed over to the GWR.

The period of austerity after the war saw little if any improvement work undertaken but, during the 1950s, the station underwent a certain amount of modernisation. In 1953 Brunel's old booking hall on Platform No 1 was rebuilt and, in 1958, a new barrier screen, bearing the coats of arms of the various counties served by the Western Region, was erected on the 'Lawn' area and across the ends of Platforms Nos 1-8.

During 1954 Paddington celebrated its centenary and on 29 May 1954 a commemorative tablet was unveiled on Platform No 1 to mark the event. On 3 November 1961 a new enquiry centre near the entrance to Platform No 1 was opened by the Chairman of the Western Area Board, Mr R. F. Hanks.

During August 1962 Closed Circuit Television train information was introduced for the first time with four 27in monitors placed at strategic points

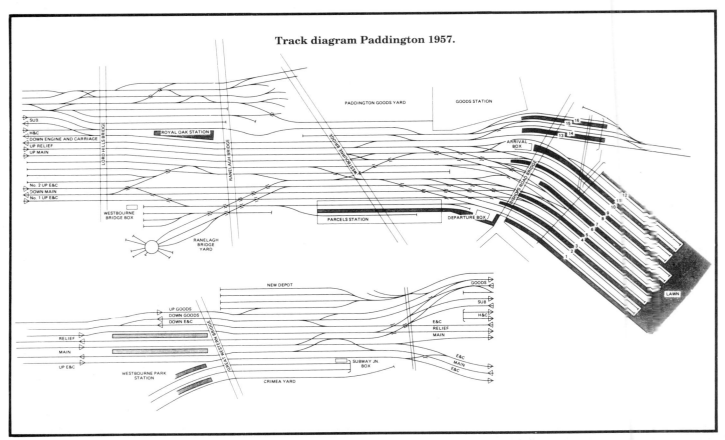

Track diagram Paddington 1957.

around the station. The introduction by the Western Region of the 24hr clock also saw all clocks at Paddington modified. During the same year the trainshed roof was repainted, and during the preparation it was found that over the years between 30 and 40 coats of paint had been applied. The earliest of these showed that, when built, the station had been painted terracotta and grey, and it was decided that the station would be painted in these colours instead of the more familiar chocolate and cream.

The withdrawal of steam traction from the Western Region in 1965 coincided with the announcement of a £2,000,000 modernisation scheme at Paddington. In order to minimise disruption, the work was carried out in nine stages between September 1967 and May 1968. The work entailed closing half the station at a time with trains being diverted to either Kensington or Marylebone.

One of the problems with the existing track layout at Paddington was the

fact that Platforms Nos 1-4 could be used only for departure traffic, and Platforms Nos 7-11 only for arrivals. The subsequent track remodelling and resignalling work now allowed two-way working into all platforms. At Bishop's Road, Platforms Nos 15 and 16 became part of the London Transport network, being used for electric services only. At Platforms Nos 13 and 14 the electrified lines were removed and converted to terminal platforms for use by suburban DMUs. On 4 October 1967 a new panel was opened at Old Oak Common box to control the new Paddington layout. During 1970 the roof was extensively refurbished. This involved the removal of the original glazing and its replacement with sheets of translucent fibreglass reinforced plastic. The work, which also included painting the remainder of the roof, cost in excess of £200,000.

Further improvements took place in 1982 when the 'Lawn' area was extended westwards. This involved the shortening of Platforms Nos 1-8 by approximately 37m, which in turn increased the size of the Lawn by about 35%.The extra space now allowed the repositioning of the arrival/destination indicator and the provision of several small shops.

To commemorate the completion of the new work a bronze statue of Brunel was unveiled on the 'Lawn' on 26 May 1982 by the Lord Mayor of Westminster, Thomas Whipham. The statue, by sculptor John Doubleday, was presented by the Bristol & West Building Society.

From soon after its opening in 1854 Paddington had housed the headquarters of the Great Western Railway and latterly the Western Region. However, on 13 February 1984 this ended when the Western Region headquarters were moved 77 miles west to new offices at Swindon.

On 1 October 1984 a new Red Star parcels depot was opened adjacent to the station in London Street. This is fully mechanised and currently deals with several thousand parcels each day. On 6 January 1986 the old 'Solari' train indicator was removed from the 'Lawn' area and replaced by the electronic indicator that is still in use today. From 7 October 1985 the open station system was introduced at Paddington, although ticket barriers are still retained for suburban passengers.

During 1988 a start was made on the £4.5 million refurbishment of the station roof and at the time of writing (March 1993) this work is still in progress. Passenger numbers at Paddington have grown by some 25% over the last few years and, in March 1992, work was started on a £40 million modernisation project which will take Paddington into the 21st century. Current developments are dealt with in Chapter 14.

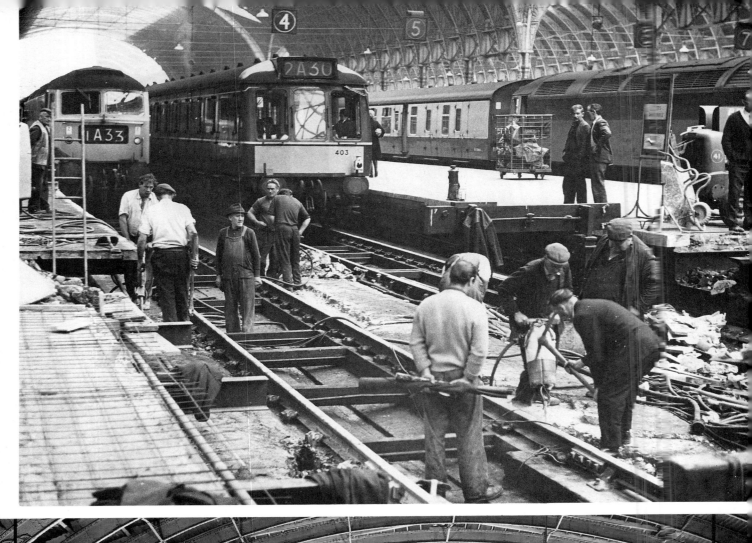

Facing page, top:
In 1968 the 'Lawn' area at Paddington was increased by extending the concourse westwards. Work is in progress in this view taken on 1 November 1968. *John H. Bird*

Facing page, bottom:
The interior of the train shed at Paddington on 20 June 1970, showing the new 'sodium' type lights that had been recently installed. *Ian Allan Library*

Above:
Unfortunately the popular Class 50s have now all been withdrawn from passenger duties. For many years they formed the mainstay of the Oxford and Newbury line services. Pictured at Paddington on 31 May 1987 is No 50044 *Exeter* with the 11.15am service from Oxford. *Brian Morrison*

The genius surveying his railway. Since 1982 this statue of Brunel, by the sculpture John Doubleday, has stood on the Lawn at Paddington. *Author*

8. The Great Western Hotel Paddington

The first suggestion for a hotel at Paddington seems to have been made by James St John Burke who wrote to the Great Western in November 1850 suggesting that a large hotel should be added to the proposed new station. The GW obviously took notice, for, as stated earlier, at a company board meeting in February 1851 it was decided 'to agree for building on the Company's property an Hotel with refreshment rooms, dormitories, stables, and other conveniences adjoining the Paddington Station'.

The hotel eventually cost some £59,500 to construct, which was quite a sum in those days. It was the first of the big railway hotels in London and was built to rival the facilities of the great continental hotels. The building was designed by Brunel and Philip Charles Hardwick and was constructed in the style of Louis XVI. It was placed across the head of the station in Praed Street to form a superb architectural frontispiece. It is, however, open to conjecture as to just how much input Brunel had in the design of the building. (Incidentally, Praed Street is named after

Drawing showing the frontage of the Great Western Hotel. *Great Western Trust*

William Praed, a banker and first chairman of the Grand Junction Canal Co.)

The hotel was opened for business on 9 June 1854 and reports at the time state that it was inspected on the same day by Prince Albert, the Prince of Wales and the King of Portugal. It has been suggested that the hotel was officially opened by the King of Portugal but the author can find no official verification of this. It is quite probable however that 'glasses were raised' to the success of the hotel and that the inspection prompted the Great Western to use the term 'Royal Hotel'.

The new hotel was certainly an impressive building, with its seven

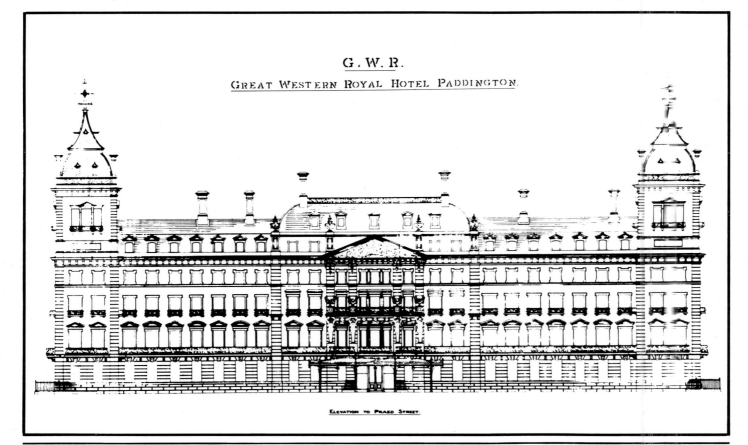

G.W.R.
GREAT WESTERN ROYAL HOTEL PADDINGTON.

ELEVATION TO PRAED STREET.

floors containing 112 bedrooms. There were also 15 sitting rooms — many of which were suites — and various other public rooms. A novel feature at the time was that all the corridors and staircases were fireproof. The pediment on the frontage was sculpted by John Thomas and depicts Britannia surrounded by representations of peace, plenty, industry and science. The hotel was originally connected to the station by a series of footbridges, with luggage being transferred from the hotel and across the Lawn to the departure platforms using specially constructed rail mounted trolleys. However, over the years the footbridges gradually fell out of use and were removed during the 1930s.

Because of the hotel's size the GW had difficulty in finding anyone to run it, so it was leased to the Great Western Hotel Co. This was actually a subsidiary company of the railway formed by some GW officers and shareholders. Brunel himself, was one of the directors and very soon became the first chairman. The Great Western Hotel Co lasted until 1896, when its 42-year lease on the building finally expired. The hotel was subsequently taken over and run by the railway itself.

The first GW restaurant cars were introduced during May 1896 and, at the time, the catering department was unable to service them, so, until January 1898 the cars were supplied with provisions from the hotel.

Over the years the building has undergone much modernisation.

Hand bill announcing the hotel opening, complete with tariffs. *Great Western Trust*

Records show that electric lighting was first installed in 1886 and that around the turn of the century the hotel was fitted with electric lifts to all floors. During 1906 the hotel was fitted with central heating and on 9 July of the same year a 400-extension telephone exchange was opened at the hotel, enabling each of the bedrooms and public rooms to be provided with its own telephone. During 1914 the hotel was fitted for the first time with electrically-operated cold storage facilities.

In 1936 the GW undertook an extensive refurbishment of the hotel. This included the provision of a new east wing containing a lounge, smoke room, cocktail bar and 52 bedrooms each with own bathroom. The existing kitchens were completely modernised, and the west wing of the hotel was also refurbished, with all bedrooms being provided with en suite bathrooms. At the same time all the floors in this section

The Great Western Royal Hotel pictured here around the turn of the century. The building, which was designed by Brunel and Hardwick, was opened on 9 June 1854. This picture shows to good effect the covered 'Lawn' area between the hotel and the station. The small kiosk on the left is the Great Western Railway enquiry office. *Great Western Trust*

GREAT WESTERN ROYAL HOTEL.

The above new Hotel, connected with the Paddington Station, was opened for business on Friday last, the 9th instant.

These premises have been built by the Company, and are fitted up with every modern convenience for Families as well as for Single Persons, while the Terms have been fixed for every description of Hotel Business upon a very moderate Scale of Charge.

Parties are strongly recommended to order their Apartments previously, by letter, addressed to Mr. Wheeler, Manager, Great Western Royal Hotel, Paddington Station, who is authorised to enter into arrangements for the reception of Parties for a given time at a rate of charge by the Week or the Day.

Passengers by the Trains can pass between the Platforms and the Hotel at once, without trouble or expense, and proper persons will be always in attendance to receive and carry the Luggage to or from the Trains.

TARIFF.

GROUND FLOOR.—Sitting Room, per day, 6s.; Small sitting room, 4s.

LARGE APARTMENTS ON FIRST FLOOR.—Drawing Room and Two Bed Rooms (with Water Closet enclosed) *en suite*, per day, 22s. 6d ; Drawing Room and Two Bed Rooms, 20s ; Drawing Room and Bed Room, 15s.; Bed Room and Dressing Room, 10s.; Single Bed, 5s.

SECOND FLOOR.—Sitting Room, per day, 7s. 6d.; Large Bed Room, 3s. 6d.; Small Bed Room, 2s. 6d.

THIRD FLOOR.—Large Bed Room, per day, 2s. 6d.; Small Bed Room, 2s.

FOURTH FLOOR.—Large Bed Room, per day, 2s.; Small Bed Room, 1s. 6d. Except the Suites, 1s. extra will be charged when the Bed is occupied by Two Persons.

EXTRAS.—Sitting Room Fire, 1s. 6d.; Bed Room Fire 1s.; Breakfast with Eggs, 2s.; Breakfast with Cold Meat or Chop, 2s. 6d.; Breakfast with Broiled Ham and Eggs, 3s.

COFFEE ROOM DINNERS, &c.—Joint and Plain Vegetables, 2s. 6d.; Chops. 2s.; Steaks, 2s ; Cold Meat, 2s.; Basin of Soup, 1s.; Sandwich, 6d.; Cup of Tea, 6d.; Cup of Coffee, 6d. Visitors' Servants' Meals, 4s. per day; Hot Baths, 2s. 6d.; Cold Baths, 1s. 6d.

WINES.—Draught Port, per pint, 2s. 6d., per bottle, 5s.; Old Bottled Port, 3s. and 6s.; Very Old Port, 3s. 6d. and 7s.; Draught Sherry, 2s. 3d. and 4s. 6d.; Golden Sherry, 2s. 6d. and 5s.; Brown Sherry, (East India,) 3s. and 6s.; Pale Sherry, (East India,) 3s. 6d. and 7s.; Amontillado, 4s. and 6s.; Madeira, 3s. and 6s.; Old East India, 8s. per bottle; Champagne, per pint, 4s. and per bottle, 7s. 6d.; Claret, (Johnson's,) 8s. 6d. per bottle; Claret (Johnson's,) 7s. 6d.; Chateaux Margaux, (Johnson's,) 6s.; St. Julien, (Johnson's,) 5s. 6d.; Medoc, (Johnson's,) 4s.

SPIRITS AND LIQUEURS.—Brandy, per glass, 1s.; Hollands, 1s.; Rum, 6d.; Gin, 6d.; Whiskey, 9d.; Maraschino, 1s.; Curacco, 1s.; Noyeau, 1s.; Orange Brandy, 1s.; Liqueur Brandy, 1s.; Cherry Brandy, 1s.; Eau de Vie de Danzic, 1s.

ALE AND STOUT.—Allsopp's Pale Ale, per pint 6d., per bottle 1s.; Scotch, 6d. and 1s.; Burton, 6d. and 1s.; Stout, 6d and 1s.; Cyder, 6d and 1s.; Soda-Water, 6d. per bottle; Brighton Seltzer, 9d.; Lemonade, 6d.; Carrara Water, 6d.

HOTEL ARRANGEMENTS.—The Servants of the Establishment are not allowed to receive any Fees or Gratuities whatever from the Visitors; but, in lieu thereof, 1s. 6d. will be charged to each Visitor for attendance for the first day, and 1s. per day afterwards. Visitors not having Apartments in the Hotel will be charged 6d. attendance for each meal. The charge for attendance includes the removal of Luggage to and from the Hotel, and for all services rendered throughout the Establishment. The Proprietors will not be responsible for any property lost in the Hotel unless given in charge of the Superintendent. Visitors may lock up their Rooms during their absence, giving the key in charge of the Superintendent.

were fireproofed. A new carriage way and entrance hall were also constructed. The finishing touches saw the hotel frontage cleaned and smartened up. The new work was finished and formally inaugurated on Thursday 13 March 1938 by the Chairman of the company, Sir Robert (later Viscount) Horne. It has been difficult to pinpoint the exact date, but it was probably during World War 2, that the ornate railings were removed from around the front of the hotel.

With the nationalisation of the railways in 1948, the hotel became part of the British Transport Hotels Group. Since then, the hotel has been refurbished on several occasions. During the 1950s much of the ornate wood panelling in the public areas was renewed, and during the early 1960s the entrance lobby was modernised and the interior was redecorated.

The hotel was sold by British Transport Hotels in the 1980s, and is now in private ownership. The current owners have recently completed an extensive refurbishment programme. The latest work, which cost some £6,000,000, was completed in the spring of 1991 and has provided the hotel with the most up to date facilities. These include a new business and conference centre together with 17 separate business suites. All of the bedrooms have been restyled and fitted with televisions and radios. The restaurant, carvery and brasserie have all been updated. Today the Hotel is as busy as ever and continues to form a fine frontage to Brunel's 'Gateway to the West'.

Advert from the 1939 Great Western timetable. *Great Western Trust*

9. Passenger Services

The first Great Western passenger train left Paddington for Maidenhead at 8am on Monday 4 June 1838. This first service carried some 200 passengers and took, according to Gibbs, 1hr 20min to cover the 22½ miles. The first up service left Maidenhead also at 8am. There were initially eight services in each direction daily. No official timetables were published for these first trains but, instead, services were advertised in local newspapers (the first timetable proper was not published until 1 May 1839). The reason for this was explained by Saunders in a report dated April 1841: 'At the opening in 1838 we found the engines were so inefficient that time-table working was hopeless; one or two engines might keep time, the other eight or ten were always out of time. So we suspended time-tables till the locomotive power became sufficient'. What is particularly interesting is that even when timetables were issued no times were given for the intermediate stations, again due to the unreliability of the locomotives. The problem is again illustrated in this extract from a report by the Traffic Superintendent, Seymour Clark, of the situation on 7 June 1839: 'We are badly off again for engines. The *North Star* broke her cranked axle at Drayton engine house. The *Thunderer* is as you know damaged; the *Hurricane* is in dock; and the *Lion* with the levers of her weigh bar broken. The *Morning Star* has a cylinder split and the cover gone. We have the *Atlas*, the *Eagle*, the *Ajax* the three small Vulcans (*Apollo*, *Neptune* and *Venus*) and the *Vulcan*. The *Apollo* is on the short train, the *Venus* and *Neptune* working together. The trains have been later in consequence of these accidents.'

Also there does not appear to have been any particular requirement for trains to keep to the proper road! Gibbs records that on 26 September 'the 8 o'clock train ran into an experimental train this morning and injuring three of the carriages very much'. Gooch himself, in later years remarked: 'It was a marvel to me we escaped serious accidents. It was no uncommon thing to take an engine to look for a late train out on the line'. If the train was sighted a hurried reversal took place in order to avoid a collision. However, this rather cavalier attitude to running did not seem to affect the overall traffic and, by the end of the year, some 26,644 passengers had been carried, producing receipts for the company of £43,845. In 1839 when the line had been opened through to Twyford the figure had risen to 606,396 passengers and by the end of the following year the figure had topped a million. Trains at this time usually comprised three open seconds (216 passengers) and three firsts (96). At first the company refused to carry third-class passengers, or as they were termed at the time 'persons from the lower stations of life', but during 1839 a local Twyford carrier was advertising third-class travel for just 3s 6d (17.5p). The only snag was that the unfortunate passengers had to travel in an open goods wagon. By the time the railway was opened to Reading the GW itself was advertising third-class travel: 'The goods train passengers will be conveyed in uncovered wagons by goods trains only; 14lbs of luggage allowed to each, all access is charged at the usual rate for passenger's luggage'.

This appalling contempt by the company for the lower classes resulted in many 'fatalities whilst in conveyance', and it was to take Gladstone's Railway Regulation Act of November 1844 to stop the practice. This act compelled all railway companies (for the GW was not the only culprit) to provide seats and

Old Oak Lane Halt was opened on 1 October 1906 and was situated on the 'new line' about a quarter mile from Old Oak Common Junction. The halt is pictured here in c1931. It was finally closed on 30 June 1947. *L&GRP*

proper covered accommodation for their passengers, to run at least one stopping train daily in each direction at a speed of not less than 12mph including stops, and to charge only one penny a mile. These were known as 'Parliamentary' trains

Looking at the timetables of this period it is interesting to note that they carry a reference to 'local time'. The 1841 timetable, for example, mentions that 'London Time is kept at all stations on the railway, which is about four minutes earlier than Reading time; 5½ minutes before Steventon time; 7½ minutes before Cirencester time; 8 minutes before Chippenham time; 11 minutes before Bath and Bristol time and 14 minutes before Bridgwater time'. The explanation of this is that each one degree of Longitude west represents about four minutes in time from Greenwich and with the GW lines travelling west the change in Longitude made quite a difference to the local time. Standard Time (Greenwich Mean Time) was adopted from Sunday 18 November 1883 but, prior to this, London time was conveyed down the line initially by the first down train each day and from about 1852 by telegraph.

By 1842 there were 13 down services each day and two mixed goods departing from Paddington. Eight ran through to Bristol and Taunton. The remaining services ran to Slough and Reading. Up trains ran to the same pattern.

Through services between Paddington and Exeter were introduced on 1 May 1844 and on 12 June of the same year the Oxford branch was opened. Banbury was reached on 2 September

Right:
One through service using the loop ran between Ealing Broadway and Ruislip. This picture shows auto-fitted 0-6-0PT No 5418 passing Northolt East Junction box with a through Ruislip service.
C. R. L. Coles

Below right:
Another Great Western auto-fitted 0-6-0PT, No 5401, stands at Ruislip & Ickenham (now West Ruislip) with an auto service to Ealing Broadway in c1935. *C. R. L. Coles*

1850 and on 1 October 1852 services were extended through to Birmingham. For a short period some services reached Birmingham (129 miles via Oxford) in 2hr 45min, with stops only at Oxford (70min for 63½ miles) and Leamington — a remarkable schedule for that date.

The February 1868 timetable shows just 29 departures each weekday from Paddington and 12 on Sunday. Arrivals totalled 31 each weekday and 12 on Sundays.

The first major accident in the London area occurred on 24 February 1853 when an up Bristol service left the tracks at Ealing and collided with the adjacent cutting. The only passenger to be killed was James Gibbs, a director of the company on his way to a board meeting at Paddington.

The GW had introduced its first slip coaches on 29 November 1858 with coaches being detached at both Slough

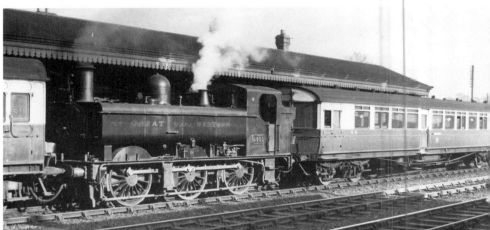

and Banbury from the 9.30am Paddington-Birmingham service. Slips were soon being made from up services. For a few months during 1864 a through coach for Kensington and Victoria was slipped from an up Bristol service at West London Junction. The 1866 service timetable for June shows a particularly unusual slip which was made from the 8.15am broad gauge service from Windsor to Moorgate Street, which ran via Bishop's Road and the Metropolitan lines to the City. It appears that this service slipped carriages at Westbourne Bridge. These were then propelled into the main arrival platform at Paddington. On reflection this was a strange manoeuvre for the service train itself stopped at Bishop's Road. These local slips were short-lived, and the Windsor slip lasted just two years. However, slip coaches became a feature of many services to and from Paddington, and by the summer of 1914 there were over 70 slip workings on the GW each day.

On 1 October 1861 standard gauge services were inaugurated between the West Midlands and Paddington, with an initial service of three trains daily in each direction. The inaugural service left Paddington at 9.45am for Birkenhead. During the same year the famous 'Flying Dutchman' service was inaugurated between Paddington and Exeter and, in 1865, the service was extended to Plymouth.

Suburban services in the London area at this time were generally provided by the longer distance services stopping en route. However, from 1 October 1863 business travellers were able to reach the City on through services from Windsor to Bishop's Road and, via the Metropolitan lines, to Farringdon Street and, from July 1866, to Moorgate. By the turn of the century these through City services had been extended to Reading, Wycombe, Maidenhead, Uxbridge and Staines.

Through services from Southall to Victoria via the West London Railway

were inaugurated on 2 March 1863 and were extended through to Windsor and Reading during the following year.

On 6 February 1873 the GW had its second serious accident in the London area when the up 'Flying Dutchman' service, travelling at between 55 and 60mph in foggy conditions, ran into the back of a goods train about half a mile east of West Drayton station. The accident was made worse when a down standard gauge Worcester service ploughed into the wreckage. Incredibly, only the front guard of the 'Dutchman' was killed and altogether just 27 passengers were injured. During the subsequent inquiry it was stated that the low casualty numbers were almost certainly

due to the stability of the broad gauge. There is no doubt that this very same reason had also contributed to the low casualty figures at the Ealing accident of 1853. It is often said that it was this accident which prompted the Board to experiment with what was to become the Automatic Train Control system.

However, the spread of the standard gauge was rapid: by 1877 of the 51 passenger trains leaving Paddington daily,

At the West Ealing end 'Western' diesel-hydraulic No D1042 *Western Princess* swings away from the main line and on to the loop with the diverted 2.10pm service from Paddington to Birkenhead on 16 December 1962. The train had been diverted due to engineering work. *M. Pope*

'County' class 4-4-0 No 3808 *County Limerick* passes Iver with an up Weymouth service on 5 August 1929. The first vehicle is a rather ancient Great Western mail van. *E. R. Wethersett*

only 12 were still using the broad gauge.

On Friday 20 May 1892 broad gauge passenger services at Paddington came to an end with the departure of the 5pm service to Plymouth. The very last up broad gauge service was the night mail that pulled into the station at approximately 5.30am on Saturday 21 May.

The first major standard gauge accident in the London area occurred on 16 June 1900 when a down fast service to the West of England collided with a Windsor train that was standing in Slough station. The driver, for no apparent reason, had apparently run through danger signals at both Dolphin Junction and Slough without slowing. Five passengers were killed and 35 were injured.

In July 1904 a new service was introduced between Paddington and Penzance. This service, which at this time ran via Bristol, was named the 'Riviera Limited' (later 'Cornish Riviera') and featured non-stop running between Paddington and Plymouth. At the time it was the longest non-stop run in the world. From 2 July 1906 it was switched to the shorter route via Castle Cary and soon took over the mantle of the GW's crack train from the 'Dutchman'. Such was the popularity of the 'Riviera' that, for many years during the summer months, it was run in up to four portions.

An interesting through service was inaugurated on Monday 2 July 1906 when the GW, together with the London, Brighton & South Coast Railway, introduced a train between Brighton and Paddington with LBSCR locomotives and rolling stock used throughout. The train left Brighton at 11.30am and travelled via Kensington (Addison Rd) to arrive at Paddington at 1.10pm. The return service left at 3.40pm and arrived back at Brighton at 5.17pm. The service, although apparently well patronised for the first few months, was not a success and was withdrawn in July 1907.

Great Western passenger services continued to grow and, in July 1910, the new cut-off route to Birmingham was

The 5.30pm service from Paddington to Plymouth hauled by 'Castle' class No 5043 *Earl of Mount Edgcumbe* passes Ruscombe in the spring of 1938.
C. R. L. Coles

opened with the introduction of several two-hour fast services between Paddington and Birmingham. However, the majority of the suburban services over the section between High Wycombe and London were operated into Marylebone using Great Central motive power and coaching stock.

During the 1930s suburban services were improved and accelerated with the introduction of new rolling stock and the new '61xx' class 2-6-2Ts. Thames Valley line services at this time comprised upwards of 25 a day in each direction between Paddington and Reading. Some of these ran into the newly reconstructed station at Bishop's Road which, from 11 September 1933, was redesignated Paddington Suburban. Through GW trains to the city were withdrawn from 16 September 1939.

On 5 February 1934 GW diesel railcars were introduced on to Thames Valley services and, by 1938, were being used on Windsor, Staines, Henley and Brentford branch services.

On 2 July 1941 an up Plymouth-Paddington service hauled by 'Castle' class No 4091 *Dudley Castle* collided head on with LMS '8F' No 8293 on a down goods near Slough. Both engines remarkably stayed upright but, unfortunately, the front coaches of the Plymouth train were badly damaged, killing five people and injuring many more.

Postwar services from Paddington actually showed little change to those before the war but, during the 1950s, the Western Region upgraded many of its principal express trains and, together with the long-running 'Cornish Riviera Express' and 'Torbay Express',

many others were also given names. The first of these 'The Red Dragon' (Paddington-Carmarthen) and 'The Inter City' (Paddington-Wolverhampton) were inaugurated in 1950, followed in 1953 with the 'Pembroke Coast Express' (Paddington-Pembroke Dock) and the 'Cheltenham Spa Express' (Paddington-Cheltenham Spa), in 1954 the 'Cambrian Coast Express' (Paddington-Aberystwyth), and in 1955 'The South Wales Pullman' (Paddington-Swansea). This was actually the first all-Pullman train to run on GW metals since the short-lived 'Torquay Pullman' service of 1929. Further namings took place with the 'Capitals United' (Paddington-Cardiff) in 1956 and the 'Cathedrals Express' (Paddington-Hereford), 'The Mayflower' (Paddington-Plymouth) and 'The Royal Duchy' (Paddington-Penzance) in 1957. To complete the upgrading, the coaching stock on many of these services was painted in the old company colours of chocolate and cream.

On 9 September 1960 an era came to an end at Paddington when the last slip coach (for Bicester) was attached to the 5.10pm service to Wolverhampton hauled by 'King' No 6001 *King Edward VII*. This was the very last slip coach working in this country.

In 1958 the first of the new North British diesel-hydraulics were introduced on to Bristol line services, and these were quickly followed by the Swindon-built 'Warships'. From 27 July 1959 many main line services, including the 'Bristolian' and 'Torbay Express', were officially diesel-hauled.

Diesel Multiple-Units had been gradually introduced on to Thames Valley and suburban services from the start of the winter 1959 timetable and, in June 1962, steam was withdrawn from Chiltern line suburban services. Also during 1962 the remaining ex-GW diesel railcars were withdrawn from Thames line services being replaced by new single-car diesel units.

The introduction of diesel traction was rapid and, by the end of 1962, the only regular Class 1 passenger services from Paddington to be steam-hauled were to Worcester and, by the end of 1965, all services from Paddington were diesel powered.

'Saint' class 4-6-0 No 2981 *Ivanhoe* runs through Taplow station with an up express from the Oxford line in c1950. The station at Taplow was built on the site of the original Maidenhead station, the 1838 terminus of the line.
R. F. Dearden

'King' class 4-6-0 No 6024 *King Edward I* passes Scrubs Lane on 29 April 1933 with a down Plymouth service. No 6024 was withdrawn in June 1962 and, after spending some years at Woodhams scrapyard in Barry, was restored by the 6024 society. It is currently kept at Didcot Railway Centre, Oxfordshire.
E. R. Wethersett

The remarkable safety record of the Paddington-Twyford section took a battering when, on the evening of 19 December 1973, the 17.18 Paddington-Oxford service, running 12min late, was derailed at speed, adjacent to Longfield Avenue between Ealing Broadway and West Ealing. It appears that the battery cover locks were not fastened properly on Class 52 No D1007 *Western Talisman*. This resulted in the cover dropping down, demolishing a point relay box, which opened a facing crossover under the locomotive and subsequently derailed the train. Ten passengers were killed and over 50 injured. In terms of fatalities this has been the worst accident over this section to date.

In May 1974 the cut-off route via Bicester was downgraded to became a suburban-only line when all but one of the remaining through services from Paddington to Birmingham were switched to run via Oxford.

A group of spotters admire the fine lines of 'Castle' class 4-6-0 No 4082 *Windsor Castle* as it passes Scrubs Lane on 7 October 1933 with the 3.30pm service from Paddington to Penzance.
E. R. Wethersett

After many months of testing, High Speed Trains were introduced on to the Paddington, Bristol and South Wales services from the 4 October 1976. The new services cut the journey times to Bristol Temple Meads (118½ miles in just 100min), and to Cardiff (145½ miles in 111min). Both journeys include several stops. The fastest service to Bristol today reaches Parkway (111¾ miles), in just 76min. On 14 May 1979 HSTs were also introduced on to the southwest services between Paddington and Exeter/Plymouth. They were soon extended through to Penzance and in August of the same year the last locomotive-hauled 'Cornish Riviera' ran.

Also during 1979 some Paddington-Birmingham services were extended to run through to Manchester and Liverpool and in 1982 a through Paddington-Glasgow service was introduced. However, this was short-lived and, from 1984, it was switched to run from Poole. For the summer 1987 timetable a through service was introduced between Paddington and Llandudno but this was not a success and lasted just one season.

In this section I have described several accidents and, at the time of writing, the last to occur took place at Paddington itself. At approximately 6.10am on Wednesday 23 November 1983, what could have been a far worse accident than any of the others was averted when Class 50 No 50041 *Bulwark* hauling the 'Night Riviera'

sleeping car service from Penzance was derailed as it approached Paddington. The locomotive, which apparently was travelling at between 40 and 50mph at the time, was derailed and slid on its side for over 100yd before colliding with the ramp end of Platform No 8 directly under the Bishop's Road bridge. Although several of the coaches were also derailed, remarkably there were only a few minor injuries. The driver cited brake failure as the cause and one can only conjecture as to what might have happened if the derailment had not taken place and the train had entered the terminus at that speed.

This chapter can only summarise the growth of the services over the years and more recent developments are covered in the chapter on the line today.

Left:
The '15xx' class 0-6-0PTs were used for many years on ECS working in and out of Paddington. Here, on 8 May 1962, No 1504 passes Westbourne Park station with stock for a down Cardiff service. Notice the pilot number (5) on the front buffer beam of the engine. *Ian Allan Library*

Centre left:
'Castle' class 4-6-0 No 5056 *Earl of Powis* accelerates past Old Oak Common West box with a down West of England service on 27 March 1961. *B. J. Jackson*

Bottom:
The 10.42am stopping service from Reading to Paddington restarts from Iver on Saturday 20 June 1961. This was a regular working at this time for a pair of '61xx' class 2-6-2Ts which, on this occasion, were Nos 6136 and 6125. *D. Cross*

Facing page, top:
The 3.45pm service from Paddington to Fishguard Harbour hauled by 'Britannia' No 70027 *Rising Star* is seen at West Ealing on 1 June 1956. In the background is the West Ealing signalbox closed on 18 March 1968. Also in view is the small milk platform (left). *R. E. Vincent*

Facing page, bottom:
Ex-Great Western 'Grange' class No 6870 *Bodicote Grange* on the 2.3?pm Paddington-Bristol (via Devizes) service passes 0-6-0PT No 9704 on a Smithfield goods service at Acton West Junction on 30 June 1956. *R. C. Riley*

'Castle' class 4-6-0 No 7012 *Barry Castle* pictured here at West Ealing on 10 April 1954 with the down 'Pembroke Coast Express', the 10.55am service from Paddington to Pembroke Dock.
C. R. L. Coles

Crossing at speed near Maidenhead on 16 May 1954 are 'Hall' No 5938 *Stanley Hall* and 'Castle' No 5039 *Rhuddlan Castle*. *J. F. Russell-Smith*

'Hall' class No 4948 *Northwick Hall* on a Henley-Paddington special is about to be overtaken by 'Castle' No 5020 *Trematon Castle* on the up 'Red Dragon' service near Twyford on 5 July 1951.
Brian Morrison

The up 'Cathedrals Express' hauled by 'Castle' No 7027 *Thornbury Castle* speeds through Iver station in July 1961. *M. Pope*

The 8.20am service from Neyland to Paddington hauled by 'Britannia' Pacific No 70027 *Rising Star* passes the Grand Union Canal at West Drayton on 17 August 1957. It was around this spot that the Great Western's first two engines, *Vulcan* and *Premier*, were delivered by canal in November 1837. *K. L. Cook*

Top:
Swindon-allocated Standard Class 5 No 73022 passes Old Oak Common East box with a down stopping service on 12 October 1957. *R. C. Riley*

Above:
An Ealing Broadway-Greenford DMU service stands at Platform No 3 at West Ealing on 15 July 1960. *British Rail*

Right:
The 9.45pm service from Paddington to Weston-Super-Mare hauled by 'Warship' No D856 *Trojan* speeds past Bryce, White & Co's wood yard at Slough on 4 February 1964. *G. J. Jefferson*

Left:
For a short while in the late 1960s some of the West of England services were double-headed using 'Warship' class diesel-hydraulics as illustrated in this picture of Nos D823 *Hermes* and D870 *Zulu* approaching Slough on 11 June 1969 with the up 'Cornish Riviera Express'. Also in shot is the goods shed, opened in the 1930s, and the Horlicks factory. *J. H. Cooper-Smith*

Below:
The up 'Bristol Pullman' runs past the large goods shed at Paddington New Depot (Westbourne Park) on 21 August 1969. The first Paddington New Depot, a much smaller affair, was opened on 13 April 1908 and stood on the site of the old Westbourne Park engine sheds. It was rebuilt and enlarged in the 1930s as seen in this picture. It was closed on 29 December 1972 and today sees partial use as a Topmix cement terminal and as the headquarters and garage area for a London cab company. *J. H. Cooper-Smith*

Right:
This view from the footbridge at Southall on 2 March 1974 shows two Class 52 'Western' diesel-hydraulics at speed. On the left is No D1045 *Western Viscount* bearing the 09.55 service from Paignton to Paddington passing, on the right, No D1043 *Western Duke* on the 13.30 service from Paddington to Penzance. *G. F. Gillham*

Experimental Class 210 diesel-electric unit No 210002 passes Acton Wells junction on 31 March 1983 with the 15.35 stopping service to Slough. *Michael J. Collins*

Class 47 No D1913 near the West London Sidings on 4 July 1968 with the down substitute 'Bristol Pullman' service during the NUR go-slow. The ECS line from Old Oak can be seen in the background. *J. H. Cooper-Smith*

Top left:
The 16.45 service to Bristol Temple Meads hauled by Class 47 No 1949 passes the stabling point at Ranelagh yard on 16 May 1973. On the left background is the Westway road and, at rail level, the island platform at Royal Oak. The three railway bridges in view are Ranelagh Bridge, Westbourne Bridge and, in the far background, Bishop's Road. *Brian Morrison*

Bottom left:
The view looking west shows Type 4 No D1307 arriving with the 12.10 Worcester service. The picture is undated but is taken prior to the 1967 track alterations. Notice the small water tank. This was used in steam days to replenish shunting engines. At this time the goods depot (left) is still very much in use. *Colin Gifford*

Right:
HST set No 253030 winds its way out of Paddington on 25 February 1984 with the 11.05 service to Bristol. Standing at Platform No 1A are Class 47 No 47500 *Great Western* and Class 50 No 50007 *Sir Edward Elgar*, both in green livery. *Brian Morrison*

Above:
Class 50 No 50006 *Neptune* runs alongside the Grand Union Canal at Kensal Green on 17 August 1985 with empty coaching stock for Old Oak. Kensal Green Gasworks can be seen on the left centre. *Michael J. Collins*

Right:
For many years the Class 50s formed the main motive power on Oxford line services. Here, on 3 August 1983, No 50009 *Conqueror* passes the closed goods depot at Paddington as it leaves with the 13.10 service to Oxford. *C. Addis*

Below:
A pair of Class 50s Nos 50036 *Victorious* and 50038 *Formidable* speed past the Plasser Railway Machinery works at Hanwell with the 10.19 service from Newbury to Paddington. *Hugh Ballantyne*

Class 50 No 50034 *Furious*, with empty stock from the Penzance-Paddington sleeper service, approaches Acton West *en route* to Willesden, via the Greenford Loop, on 7 July 1986. At this time the sleeping cars were being serviced at Stonebridge Park. *Colin J. Marsden*

Many of the Great Western/Great Central joint line suburban services were operated using ex-LNER stock, as illustrated by ex-GC Class 'A5/1' 4-6-2T No 69814 as it traverses the joint section near Tylers Green on 6 June 1953 with a Princes Risborough-Marylebone service. *Brian Morrison*

Top:
The 7.20am service from Pwllheli to Paddington runs through Beaconsfield on 2 August 1958 hauled by 'Castle' No 5026 *Criccieth Castle*. *J. D. Edwards*

Above:
'Castle' class 4-6-0 No 5022 *Wigmore Castle* approaches Old Oak Common West Junction with the 6.45pm service from Wolverhampton to Paddington on 4 May 1957. In the foreground is the Central line and top left, under the bridge, North Acton station. *R. C. Riley*

Right:
The impressive sight of 'King' class 4-6-0 No 6006 *King George I* as it speeds through West Ruislip station in July 1949 with an up service from Birkenhead to Paddington. *C. R. L. Coles*

'Hall' class No 4977 *Watcombe Hall* runs under the signal gantry at South Ruislip in May 1956 with the 4.10pm service from Paddington to Wolverhampton. On the right is the Central line extension and, in the background, Northolt Junction West box. Today the whole of this line is signalled from Marylebone.
C. R. L. Coles

An unidentified 'Hall' on an up Wolverhampton express passes ex-GC 'A5' class 4-6-2T No 5045 on a High Wycombe-Marylebone service at Gerrards Cross in July 1947.
C. R. L. Coles

10. The Goods Department

Although it was always the Great Western's intention to carry goods, it was not until September 1839 that the first goods trains ran from Paddington to the then terminus of the line at Twyford. From the opening of the line the Great Western had been running a nightly coke train between London and Twyford and it was on this service that the first goods were carried. At first the goods service was operated by carriers. Prices for general goods were 15s per ton or 9s per hundredweight, beasts 10s per head; calves, sheep and pigs were priced at 2s 6d, 1s and 1s 8d respectively.

On 4 February 1840 the GW established a night mail service between Paddington and Twyford, a service that also carried passengers. I suppose one could argue for and against mail and parcels being included in the general goods category but there is no doubt that the expansion of this traffic provided a considerable percentage of the company's overall goods receipts for many years.

The first four sorting carriages were ordered by the Postmaster General in July 1841 and, in addition, four second-class carriages were converted to carry day mail bags and their guard, sheltered from the weather. On 1 February 1855 the first postal service was introduced between Paddington and Bristol. This, incidentally, was the first such service anywhere. The down 'Special Mail' service ran every night including Sundays and initially comprised two sorting carriages and a van. The service left London at 8.46pm with the corresponding up service leaving Bristol at 12.35am. By the 1860s some form of collecting apparatus was in use, as mentioned in the following note from a working timetable of the period: 'Bags are exchanged by means of the apparatus at Southall, West Drayton, Slough, Taplow, Twyford, Cholsey Bridge, Challow and Shrivenham'.

During the first year mail and parcels traffic produced a total revenue of just £1,366 but by 1870 it had grown to some £250,000, and by the turn of the century to £1.5 million.

Surprisingly the GW was quite slow to exploit the potential for general goods traffic, for, in 1841, when the line was opened through to Bristol there were just two goods trains each day between each location. However, a company report dated February 1842 states 'already some quantities of coal and stone are brought for conveyance by railway, and it is anticipated that these two articles alone will add considerably to the revenue of the company'. At this time goods receipts totalled £25,845 and accounted for just 3% of the company revenue. Gradually, however, the system expanded and by 1850 the goods service was carrying over 350,000 tons of merchandise and producing an annual revenue of £202,978, which represented some 24% of the annual turnover. Up to this time goods services came under the traffic department and it was not until about 1850 that the Great Western appointed its first separate goods manager. This was obviously a good move for, by 1870, the revenue from goods traffic had risen to £2,218,998 which represented 52% of the company's annual turnover.

This general view shows the Great Western Goods depot at Paddington pictured here in 1932 and shortly before reconstruction work began. The roof appears to have been added to at various times. Notice also the newly completed platform No 1A to the left.
Great Western Trust

This photo shows horses being led down the ramp entrance to the Great Western Mint stables at London Street, Paddington. Some 500 horses were kept at Paddington and each horse had its own stable and keeper. *Great Western Trust*

By the 1870s goods traffic in the Paddington area was mainly using the standard gauge. The working timetable for January 1878 shows just two regular broad gauge goods services, both running between London and Bristol.

The first goods station was opened at Paddington in around 1840. The shed which was constructed of wood, measured 330ft long and 120ft wide and contained two 11ft wide platforms. It stood on the eastern side of the Bishop's Road bridge and on the site of the present station. A few goods sidings, served by a traverser, were situated just to the west of the shed and adjacent to the road bridge. Various cranes and other equipment were dotted about the yard. Records show that in 1845 the goods superintendent at Paddington was a Mr W. Massey. The goods shed was closed and demolished during 1853 to make room for the new station.

A new goods depot was opened on the site of the old passenger station at Bishop's Road in around 1858. The new shed was constructed using cast-iron

Right
Four horses of the cartage department pose for the photographer alongside the goods building at Paddington probably around the turn of the century. Judging by the way the wagon is loaded these horses certainly had to earn their keep. *Great Western Trust*

with wooden cladding. Its rather irregular shape contained several platforms with room under its glazed roof for up to 300 wagons. The offices, unusually, stood on supports in the centre of the shed. A large goods warehouse stood adjacent to the Harrow Road but this was partially burnt down around the turn of the century. Within the depot were some 16 tracks, each connected via a series of small wagon turntables. Two of these tracks ran through to the back of the depot on a brick viaduct to a small yard. This was connected, via a series of truck lifts, to the high level yard which ran alongside the Grand Junction Canal. Road transport at this time was in the hands of the 'Cartage Department' and was operated using horses. Over 500 horses were used at Paddington and these were kept at the Great Western Mint stables at South Wharf Road. This large three-storey

A mixture of horse and mechanical transport at Paddington Goods in c1925. *Great Western Trust*

Paddington Goods offices pictured here on 25 July 1946. The offices were constructed alongside the Bishop's Road bridge. The low level entrance to the goods depot can be seen in the left centre of the picture. *Ian Allan Library*

building was probably constructed around 1860. Stabling was on all three floors, reached by a series of ramps, and each horse had its own stall. Other facilities included a farrier's shop and a room for the repair of harnesses. The horses employed at Paddington were specially bred and were known as the London Van Horse. They were generally lighter and more active than the Shire horses and were considered by the company to be more suited to the London streets. Fodder was dispatched from the Provender Store at Didcot at the rate of 1,100 sacks a week. Sick horses were

treated at both Paddington and Westbourne Park with a large recuperation field being provided at Castle Bar, West Ealing. The company also kept horses at both Poplar and Victoria and Albert docks and it appears that these were also supplied from the Paddington Mint Stables. It is not completely clear exactly when the mint stables were closed but I believe that part of the building was still in use up to c1950, although the last cartage horse was not retired from Paddington until 1954.

During the 1870s two new goods yards were opened by the GW in the London area. The first of these, opened in January 1877, at Acton was followed by a yard at Old Oak Common in June 1879. Both yards were primarily used for coal traffic.

Coal has always been an important commodity for the railways. It was first carried by the GW, albeit in small

amounts, soon after the opening of the line, but by 1846 some 4,350 tons per month was being transported into the capital alone. During 1856 the GW signed an agreement with the Ruabon Coal Co for the transport of household coal to London. It was not until December 1861 when the GW took over the South Wales Railway that coal traffic became a major part of the company's revenue. The amount continued to rise and by the turn of the century over 1 million tons per year was being transported from the South Wales pits into London.

The Great Western Goods depot at South Lambeth pictured here in December 1912. The depot was officially opened on 1 January 1913. *Great Western Trust*

The expansion of goods traffic around the turn of the century saw additional sidings opened at Acton in 1901 and on the down side of the main line at Old Oak Common during 1902. The construction of the first part of the new cut-off route to Birmingham saw a new goods yard opened at Park Royal during 1906. In the same year, a small yard was also constructed adjacent to the the GW power plant at Park Royal and was used for the delivery and storage of coal for the power station. Shortly after World War 1 a large trading estate was established at Park Royal which, by the 1950s, was dealing with 246,000 tons of general merchandise and 109,000 tons of coal per annum.

In March 1906 the goods administration at Paddington was centralised with the opening of a new office block at Bishop's Road. The new offices, which measured 220ft x 41ft x 70ft high, were erected over the roadway to the goods station and high level coal yard.

Interestingly, a goods department dining club had been formed in 1875. This was originally housed in a building that stood adjacent to the passenger

station at Paddington but, in 1934, it was resited under the ramped approach road to Platform 6. The club had a membership of 1,600, and was open for 24hr a day, providing meals for up to 500 men daily.

The GW had expanded its services into the City with the opening of a new goods depot at Smithfield in 1869. This was followed by the opening of further depots, at Poplar in 1878, at Victoria and Albert Docks in 1900 and at South Lambeth in 1913.

To the West the GW constructed its own dock at Brentford, (details are covered in the Brentford branch section).

'57xx' class 0-6-0PT No 5745 stands under the lights at Paddington in 1937. On the right is the 10.10pm postal service to Penzance. *C. R. L. Coles*

The GW depot at Smithfield was fully opened on 3 May 1869, and was situated beneath the famous meat market. The depot was constructed in a huge cellar that originally had been built for use as a slaughterhouse. The depot measured approximately 600ft x 250ft and once had a workforce of some 500 men. Because of its position it was very cramped and this necessitated wagons

being moved around its six sidings using a series of 17 capstans and 25 turntables. The sidings could accommodate up to 74 wagons at a time. An additional siding provided extra storage capacity for a further 24 wagons. The depot was illuminated by gas lamps, which burned 24hr a day. Two hydraulic lifts connected the GW depot with the main market above.

Although the GW depot was essentially for the supply of chilled and fresh meat, much of which came in by special trains from Birkenhead and Liverpool, it also dealt with general merchandise including fruit and vegetables and for many years it was handling in excess of 160,000 tons of this merchandise each year.

Smithfield was served by up to 12 trains a day, eight of which arrived during the hours of darkness. They ran to and from Acton Yard via Bishop's Road, the Metropolitan tunnels, Farringdon and Aldersgate from where they reversed into the sidings. In the early days these services were hauled by members of the '633' class 0-6-0T and 2-4-0 'Metro' tanks fitted with condensing apparatus, but in 1933 these were replaced by 11 '57xx' class 0-6-0 condensing tanks Nos 9700-10. On these engines the ATC apparatus was automatically clipped to clear the live rails. They continued to work the Smithfield services until c1961 after which 0-6-0 diesel shunters were used. Trains were limited to 25 four-wheeled wagons and a guards van, due to the short signalling sections on the Metropolitan

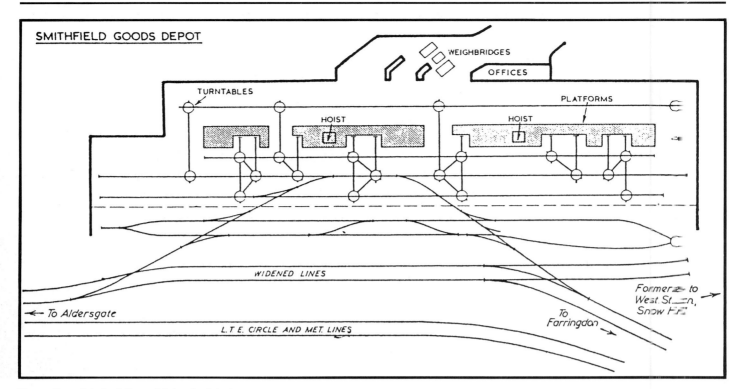

SMITHFIELD GOODS DEPOT

WEIGHBRIDGES

OFFICES

TURNTABLES

HOIST

HOIST

PLATFORMS

WIDENED LINES

← To Aldersgate

To Farringdon →

Former to West St, Snow Hill

L.T.E. CIRCLE AND MET. LINES

lines. One third of the vehicles had to be vacuum-fitted in order to give adequate braking on the sharp inclines. The very last goods service ran to Smithfield on Saturday 28 July 1962, and the depot was closed by the Western Region on 1 August 1962.

Poplar Docks Goods was opened in 1878 and was connected to the GW system at Acton with services running via the North London line. This large depot had a workforce of some 400 men and stood adjacent to the East and West India Docks. The large goods shed contained six tracks, each connected by a series of turntables and generally dealt with imports such as fresh and dried fruit, canned goods, grain and machinery. Exports mainly comprised motor cars, machinery and foodstuffs. In 1937 over 121,000 tons of merchandise passed through the depot. During the blitz Poplar Goods suffered severe bomb damage and was closed on 9 October 1940.

The GW also opened a goods depot at the Victoria and Albert Docks during 1900. This was situated further east than Poplar but was again served via the North London line from Acton. The principal commodity handled by the depot was meat with some 16,000 tons

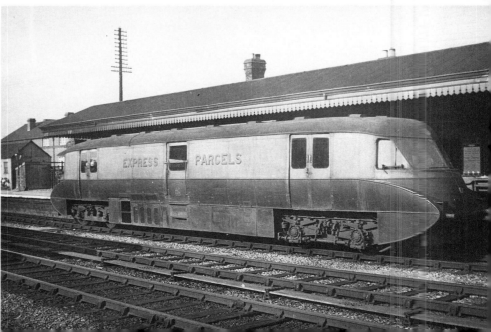

Centre right:
'Dean Goods' 0-6-0 No 2444 is seen here in the small yard at West Ruislip after arriving with the 8.30am Banbury-Old Oak pick-up goods in September 1948. *A. A. Delicata*

Right:
Great Western parcels car No 17 stands at West Ruislip on 13 October 1947. This car was allocated to Southall and was used for local parcels traffic in the London area. *A. A. Delicata*

A PW train hauled by 2-6-2T No 6107 leaves West Ruislip for Taplow in 1947.
C. R. L. Coles

being received and despatched each year. The principal export was motor vehicles. The depot also dealt with general traffic for the East London area and in the 1930s handled some 138,000 tons per annum.

The newest of the GW depots in London was at South Lambeth, and was the only GW depot south of the Thames. It was constructed on the site of the Southwark and Vauxhall Waterworks and stood between the River Thames and Stewarts Lane Junction. It was opened for milk traffic on 25 March 1911, for goods in full wagons from 5 December 1910 and was fully opened for all goods on 1 January 1913. The new depot served the southern districts of London within the Lambeth, Battersea, Brixton, Camberwell, Southwark and Wandsworth areas. GW services to and from the depot ran via Acton, the West London line and the South East & Chatham Railway low-level lines at Longhedge Junction. The large three-storey goods shed had accommodation for up to 70 wagons and was fitted with electric traversers to move these from one road to another. The main goods warehouse was fully mechanised. The goods yard had accommodation for over 400 wagons; outside the depot, which eventually covered an area of about 12½ acres, was used for general merchandise, including about a 1,000 wagon loads of hops each year for the local breweries. In September 1921 facilities at Lambeth were expanded with the opening of a large five-floor warehouse on the north side of the depot. In later years warehouse space was rented by Messrs Kelloggs, Nestles, Lever Bros and the United Glass Bottle Co. Lambeth was undoubtedly the busiest of the four 'outside'

depots with an average annual turnover of some 340,000 tons. The depot was transferred to the Southern Region on 5 February 1968 and was finally closed on 1 November 1980.

During the winter of 1879 the goods lines at Westbourne Park station were diverted to make room for an additional pair of platforms. The new loop, which was brought into use in January 1880, ran from Portobello Junction via a 35yd long tunnel, known as the 'Cape Horn' tunnel, and along the back of the then locomotive depot to give direct access to the goods yards at Paddington. The loop line appears to have been closed on the same date as the locomotive sheds — 18 March 1906.

On 13 April 1908 a new goods depot and mileage yard was opened at Westbourne Park, on the site of the old engine sheds. This was constructed of wood and was known as Paddington New Depot. During 1938 the goods depot at Westbourne was completely rebuilt, and the original wooden shed was demolished and replaced with a new brick-built transit shed and warehouse. The new shed contained a 400ft-long platform and provided over an acre of warehouse space.

One of the main commodities to be carried by the GW into London was milk. From the earliest days milk traffic, particularly from Berkshire, had formed a major part of the company's goods traffic. In fact this section of line became known to employees as 'The Milky Way'. By the turn of the century milk was being shipped into London from all over the system; a considerable

amount of this was unloaded at Paddington but, as the amount increased, new milk depots were opened at Westbourne Park in 1912 and at Paddington Goods in 1923. Other depots were also opened at Mitre Bridge, Wood Lane, West Ealing and Kensington. At this time much of the milk was being transported using churns.

However, in 1927 the GW introduced bulk milk trains using specially designed 3,000 gal capacity wagons. The first bulk service ran from the United Dairies' depot in Wootton Bassett to its London depot at Mitre Bridge. The carriage of milk in bulk soon became an important part of the GW goods traffic and within a few years the new milk trains were serving depots at Ealing, Kensington, Westbourne Park and Paddington from 11 locations in the West Country and Wales. By the 1930s over 11,000,000 gal of milk per annum were conveyed in this way. For many years these services were hauled by the large Churchward '47xx' class 2-8-0s.

The improvement in roads and the subsequent use of road tankers saw the amount of milk transported by rail decline and gradually, during the 1970s, the remaining milk depots were closed to rail traffic.

With the steady increase in trade in the period after World War 1 Paddington Goods became very busy and by the 1920s the depot was dealing with 900,000 tons of general merchandise annually, with an average of about 270 wagons inwards and 400 wagons outwards each day. Some 900 road vehicles were also passing in and out of the depot each day. It was no surprise when, in 1925, the GW decided to rebuild the depot completely.

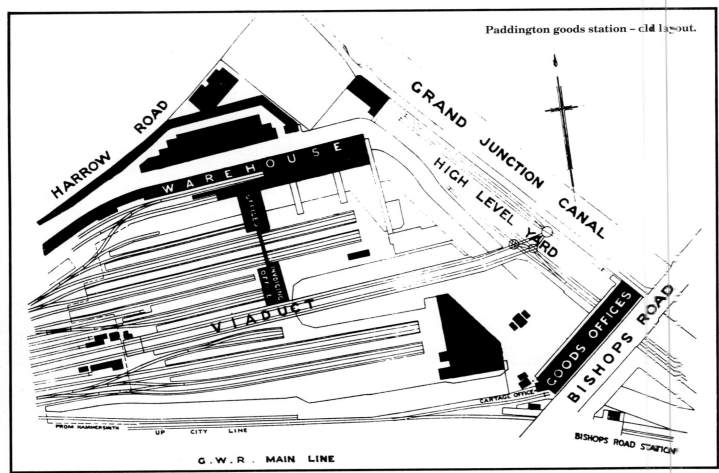

Paddington goods station – old layout.

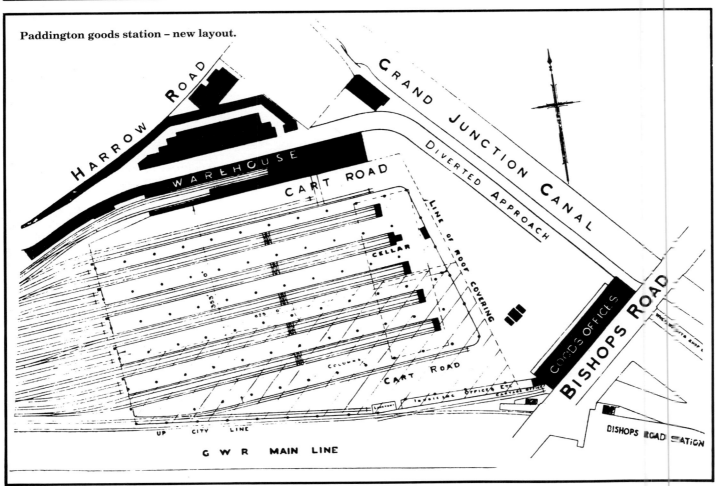

Paddington goods station – new layout.

'Star class 4-3-0 No 4062 *Malmesbury Abbey* speeds past Ealing Broadway box on 22 August 1953 with the 2.20pm Paddington-Plymouth parcels service. *S. Creer*

The new goods shed measured 625 x 353ft and contained five double-rail bays served by six platforms varying in width from 21 to 39ft. Lying at right angles to these was a large 50ft wide end platform. The roof was constructed in a series of seven spans ranging from 54 to 90ft, with the largest span covering the cart road which ran along the south side of the shed. The new shed had a capacity of about 330 wagons. In 1933 a refrigerated store was opened in the basement warehouse at Paddington Goods, and was used for the storage of lager beer. Even at this time the GW was still using horses for the majority of its short-haul delivery work in London, but for longer journeys motor transport was used. In 1932 a new maintenance depot for the company's 500 lorries, which were covering some 70,000 miles each week, was opened at Westbourne Park.

During the 1920s and 1930s considerable expansion of goods services took place in the Greater London area. On the GW system, new rail-served factory sites were opened at Acton, Hayes, Royal Oak, Southall, Langley and Slough. The largest of these was at Slough where in 1920 the Slough Trading Co (Slough Estates Ltd from 24 June 1926) set up a 650 acre trading estate on former War Department land. The War Department had opened its new Mechanical Transport Depot approximately one mile to the east of Slough station, in July 1916. The end of hostilities saw the depot used for the overhaul of surplus war vehicles for subsequent resale. Eventually the military moved out and the site was sold to the Slough Trading Co in April 1920.

For a while the Slough company continued with the refurbishment and sale of ex-WD vehicles but, at the same time, it was developing the site into a large trading estate. The estate soon proved to be very popular and, by 1935, it housed over 160 companies and contained some eight miles of sidings and a small locomotive shed for the estate's own locomotives. The trading estate also contained its own private platforms which were served, for a number of years, with special workmen's trains

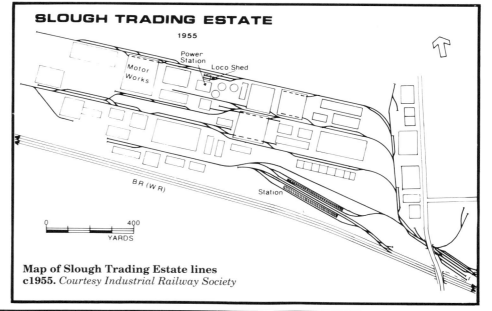

SLOUGH TRADING ESTATE

1955

Motor Works

Power Station

Loco Shed

BR (WR)

Station

0   400
YARDS

Map of Slough Trading Estate lines c1955. *Courtesy Industrial Railway Society*

from Slough and Paddington. During World War 2 part of the site was again used by the War Department as an RASC depot. Over the years the estate generated a lot of incoming and outgoing goods traffic, but gradually this was switched to road transport. By the 1960s the only service into the estate was a weekly oil train from Thames Haven which supplied the estate power station. On 27 April 1973 the remaining sidings at Slough were closed, with the power station being served via a mile long pipeline that runs from a small terminal situated on the now truncated rail entrance to the estate.

The trading estate at Park Royal also became very busy and was expanded further with the opening on 21 February 1936 of the large Guinness Brewery. Incidentally the trading estate at Park Royal was shunted for a number of years by No 13 a Sentinel 0-4-0 that was purchased by the GWR in 1926. Since 1949 Guinness has owned its own locomotives at Park Royal, and at the time of writing still operates a pair of ex-BR Class 08 shunters.

It must be remembered that a considerable amount of general goods and parcels also arrived at Paddington station. During 1933 a new parcels depot, which is still in use today, was constructed at the west end of platform No 1. This replaced the old depot that was situated alongside the 'Lawn' and had been extended in 1914. The parcels department at Paddington served an area of about 50sq miles. In the years before World War 2 the department was operating nearly 100 road vehicles and collecting and delivering up to 37,000 parcels each day. In 1927 parcel and letter handling had been made easier with the opening of the 6½-mile section of the Post Office underground railway between Paddington and Whitechapel.

Centre right:
This view shows 2-6-2T No 6132 taking water at the West Ealing milk dock after arriving with milk vans from Kensington on 29 December 1961. The milk dock at West Ealing was closed to rail traffic in c1978. Also in shot is 'Hall' No 4950 *Patshull Hall* passing on a Reading-Paddington service.
B. H. Jackson

Right:
Condensing 0-6-0PT No 9708 shunts milk empties at West Ealing on 11 March 1955. On the left is the Greenford Loop.
R. C. Riley

A down mixed goods service approaches Iver station on 11 March 1961 hauled by ex-Great Western 2-8-0 No 3814. *M. Pope*

Many other commodities were dealt with at the station. Certainly up until the late 1950s over 25,000 tons of fish per annum were unloaded at the special fish platform (No 12) and for many years large amounts of newspapers were also distributed from the station in special trains, but this traffic ceased during 1989.

The 1960s saw the opening of the first motorways with an increasing amount of goods being switched from rail to road transport. This in turn brought about a certain amount of rationalisation of goods services on the Western Region with old yards being closed. The small coal yard at Hammersmith that had been served by a daily service from Old Oak was closed on 1 February 1960. Interestingly, this service ran over the electrified lines via Bishop's Road and was generally worked using a '2251' class 0-6-0.

On 1 January 1964 a new domestic coal distribution depot was opened at West Drayton, by the National Coal Board, Stephenson Clarke Ltd and BR. The new depot, which was constructed to accept full load block trains, was built on the site of the old up yard. The new depot, which was served from both East Midlands and South Wales collieries, had a storage capacity of up to 40,000 tons. It displaced 21 former rail-served depots and yards, and was designed to have an annual throughput of up to 300,000 tons, serving an area of about 10-mile radius.

On 12 September 1966 the south goods yard at Old Oak Common was closed and during September 1973 the field sidings yard on the up side of the line suffered the same fate. Other closures during this time were the yards at Taplow in February 1965 and at Southall East in March 1965.

On 29 December 1972 the goods depot at Westbourne Park, known as Paddington New Depot, was closed and this was followed on 27 July 1975 by the depot at Slough.

The power station yard at Park Royal was closed during 1966 and in 1968 much of the main yard at Park Royal was taken out. The few remaining sidings here, apart from those serving the Guinness plant and the Marcon concrete and stone terminal, were taken out of use by 1979.

A new three-road oil terminal for the Total Oil Co was opened at Langley on

Ex-Great Western diesel parcels railcar No W34 stands at Paddington on 1 June 1951. *Brian Morrison*

21 July 1969. On 5 October 1973 the terminal was destroyed by a severe fire when the 14.40 Aldermaston-Langley service suffered a severe spillage which unfortunately ignited during unloading. The depot was subsequently rebuilt, and reopened on 29 January 1974. The 1980s also saw the reduction in use of many of the remaining yards, including Acton which was probably the busiest. A goods yard was established here in 1877, and extended around the turn of the century. A later extension was the construction of a new down yard, containing 14 sidings, which was opened on 16 November 1931. The remainder of the yard was extensively remodelled and was opened for traffic on 25 September 1932. Over the years Acton became an important exchange yard for inter-regional traffic via the North and West London lines. Under the 1960 freight plan Acton became the central yard for the Western Region London Division and by 1976 much of

the freight traffic from the Southern Region was using Acton to connect with the national freight network.

The general rundown of goods traffic during the 1980s saw the yard closed on 24 May 1984 but, surprisingly, the tracks were not removed until February 1989. A few of the up sidings were retained and today Acton is a Railfreight Construction depot, serving a Foster Yeoman stone terminal and a Redland building materials depot.

The general rundown in freight traffic also affected the large goods depot at Paddington. In August 1969 several of the sidings into the depot were removed and during 1970 the whole building was taken over by National Carriers. During December 1975 freight services into the depot were withdrawn and the depot was closed. It remained empty and unused until it was demolished in March 1986.

Above:
'2301' class 0-6-0 'Dean Goods' No 2537 runs along the Great Western main line at Twyford with a down goods on 11 June 1951. *A. R. Carpenter*

Left:
Ex-Great Western '28xx' class 2-8-0 No 2863 on an up mixed goods passes through Hanwell Station in the early 1950s. *C. R. L. Coles*

Below:
Looking resplendent in early BR lined black livery is 'Modified Hall' No 6977 *Grundisburgh Hall* seen here passing Southall with a down empty milk train on 12 April 1952. *J. C. Flemons*

Above:
'2361' class 0-6-0 No 2362 is pictured here near West Ruislip with an up goods service from Banbury on 29 June 1935.
E. R. Wethersett

Left:
One of the largest of the 'private' sidings in the area covered is at Guinness, Park Royal. The brewery was opened on 21 February 1936 and for many years the sidings were operated by a pair of Hibberd 'Plant'-type 0-4-0DMs named *Walrus* **and** *Carpenter* **which were purchased new by the company in February 1949. This picture taken in April 1975 shows the engine** *Carpenter* **at work. Both locomotives were withdrawn and replaced by a pair of ex-BR '08s' in 1985.** *Kevin Lane*

Below:
An up goods service hauled by 'Hall' class 4-6-0 No 4919 *Donnington Hall* **makes a fine sight in the winter sunshine as it passes near Slough on 4 February 1964.** *G. J. Jefferson*

One of the ex-Great Western 2-8-0 '47xx' class, No 4707, heads a down goods service through Iver station on 14 September 1962. *M. Pope*

An unidentified condensing '9700' 0-6-0PT runs through Bishop's Road station and past Paddington goods with a service from Smithfield to Acton. The five white vehicles are special meat vans. *Great Western Trust*

Ex-Great Western '2251' class 0-6-0 No 2246 runs past the small gas works (extreme right) at the West London sidings with the Paddington-Banbury pick up goods. This service stopped and shunted at every yard *en route*. *R. C. Riley*

'Manor' class 4-6-0 No 7821 *Ditcheat Manor* takes water at Ruislip Troughs as it heads an Acton-Banbury Yard goods service on 24 January 1959. 'Manors' were fairly rare visitors in the London area. *A. A. Delicata*

A down goods hauled by 2-6-2T No 6117 passes the large goods depot at Slough West on 10 October 1963. The Windsor line junction can be seen on the right of the picture. *R. C. Riley*

'Warship' (later Class 42) diesel-hydraulic No D812 *Royal Naval Reserve 1859-1959* threads its way through Slough with a down goods service on 27 May 1963. New Ford vans, manufactured in the nearby plant at Langley and transported by rail, were loaded at a small loading bay in the upside yard. *P. J. Lynch*

Not exactly on the Great Western as 'Hymek' (Class 35) diesel-hydraulic No D7059 crosses the Grand Union Canal as it traverses the West London line near Old Oak Common with a cross London goods to Acton Yard on 10 September 1966. *P. H. Groom*

Above:
The large yard at Acton pictured here on 24 April 1984 with Class 25 No 25234 on a cross-London Freight. Also in view are two of the usual three '08' pilots stationed here. This section of the yard was closed during 1985. *B. J. Beer*

Right:
Class 50 No 50034 passes beneath the North London line as it approaches North Acton with empty freightliner wagons in April 1984. *Kevin Lane*

Left:
An up parcels service hauled by 'Hymek' No D7034 is pictured here between West Ealing and Ealing Broadway on 29 May 1968. Closer examination of the trackwork shows that part of the scissors crossing from the down main to down relief has been removed.
J. H. Cooper-Smith

Above:
What is left of Acton Yard can be seen in the background as Class 47 No 47375 on a down oil train to Langley passes Class 59 No 59003 *Yeoman Highlander* on the 11.21 stone empties from Purfleet to Merehead on 18 February 1987. *Brian Morrison*

Right:
Petroleum sector Class 37 No 37887 runs off the Greenford loop at West Ealing on 30 April 1988 with the Thame-Ripple Lane oil empties. The oil depot at Thame closed in September 1991.
Alex Dasi-Sutton

Below right:
Class 31 No 31219 takes the Greenford line at West Ealing on 28 March 1985, with the Speedlink service from Acton Yard to the Guinness sidings at Park Royal. *Hugh Ballantyne*

Facing page, top:
A pair of Class 37s Nos 37294 and 37220 pass the former bitumen sidings at Thorney Mill on 10 August 1990 with the 00.01 service from Waterston to Colnbrook. *Paul D. Shannon*

Facing page, bottom:
Class 56 No 56064 runs on to the Brentford branch at Southall on 19 April 1990 with a roadstone train from Bardon Hill Quarry to Day & Sons sidings at Brentford. *Paul D. Shannon*

11. Signalling

When the line from Paddington to Maidenhead was opened the sparsity of the service allowed trains to be run purely on a time-interval system. Trains were controlled by 'policemen' who were stationed at various points along the track. However, as the services increased, so did the need for a proper signalling system. The first mention of a signal appears in the following notice issued for the opening to Twyford on 1 July 1839: 'The attention of the Engine men is called to a Signal, applied to the Level of the Switches, to denote whether they be open or shut. Two Targets are so attached that if both be seen the Switch is open, but if both range in a line so that only one can be seen, the Switch is right for the Straight Line'. The earliest mention of a fixed signal is to be found in Gooch's

Regulations for the engines working the trains on or after 30 March 1840: 'A signal ball will be seen at the entrance to Reading station when the line is right for the train to go. If the ball is not visible the train must not pass it'. However, it does appear that these balls had probably been introduced at other stations prior to this date. Disc and crossbar signals soon replaced the rather unreliable ball types and had been erected over much of the system by February 1841. However, from about 1865, the 'Disc

This picture is taken from the Great Western Magazine and shows the three-position 'American'-type signal installed just outside Paddington as an experiment in December 1914. *Great Western Trust*

and Crossbar' types were themselves replaced by the newer semaphore signals. The first of these were brought into use between Paddington and Kensal Green on 1 April 1865. According to MacDermot the first locking frame on the GW had been installed at Paddington in around 1860 'at the junction with the Metropolitan Railway'. This frame was manufactured by McKenzie & Holland and contained 25 levers. It was used to regulate up and down traffic to and from the Metropolitan line. A second 16-lever frame was also installed at Westbourne Park during the same year to control movements to and from the engine shed. The first locking frame to be constructed by the GW at its Reading Signal Works comprised 16 levers and was installed near the main departure platform at Paddington in 1863. Fur-

" Stop."	" Caution."	" Proceed."

ther improvements saw the introduction of the first fully-interlocked frame on the GW at Taplow in 1872.

The Block telegraph system of signalling was first introduced by the GW between Southall and Goring in 1870. Here the line was divided into sections with a telegraph instrument at each block post. These were then used by the 'signalmen' to send line clear or train on line information to each adjacent section.

In January 1906, audible distant signals an early form of the GW's highly successful Automatic Train Control (ATC), were installed as an experiment on the Henley on Thames branch. Although very basic in design, the system was a success. After further trials on the Fairford branch, the system was installed between Reading and Slough in November 1908 and from Slough to Paddington in 1910.

Other innovations saw a new electro-pneumatic power signalbox installed at Bath Road Junction, Slough, during 1913. The new box contained 17 levers and controlled the junction with the Windsor branch. The box at Slough was very similar in design to the power box at Didcot. (This was the first of its kind on the railway, and had been installed at Didcot North Junction in July 1905.)

In November 1914, an American-type three-position upper quadrant signal was installed at Paddington station as an experiment. The signal was the first of its kind in this country and was situated on the left side of the down main. It combined the function of a

Signalman Moriorty poses for the camera inside Friars Junction signalbox on 2 August 1931. Friars Junction box was opened on 9 March 1902 and contained a 71-lever frame. In 1953 this was removed and a new 53-lever frame was installed. The box was closed on 8 October 1962. *E. R. Wethersett*

Right:
The large 71-lever frame box at West Ealing seen on 9 August 1955. The box was fitted with a new frame and panel on 20 March 1955; the new extension can be seen on the left. It was finally closed on 18 March 1968. *Great Western Trust*

Below right:
Ex-Great Western 2-6-2T No 6167 stands at Hayes & Harlington with an up stopping service on 10 August 1958. The signalbox here was opened in December 1917 and, as can be seen, was situated to the east of the station. It was originally fitted with a 64-lever frame but this was extended to 80 levers in 1928. The box was closed on 10 June 1968. *R. C. Riley*

starter for Paddington Departure box and a distant for Westbourne Bridge. It is unclear as to when the signal was removed but it is thought that it was in use for less than a year.

The prewar reconstruction at Paddington saw all signalling on the electrified lines between Westbourne Park and Hammersmith transferred from GW control to the Metropolitan Railway on 1 January 1913. The reconstruction of the arrival platforms saw the old Arrival box replaced, on 19 April 1914, by what was said at the time to be a temporary structure. This 'temporary' box was constructed of timber and was fitted with a 70-lever frame and horizontal tappet type locking. The box was eventually replaced on 13 August 1933, during the second stage of the station rebuilding programme. It was, however, retained and used as a ground-frame controlling Platforms Nos 9-12, until it

The concrete and steel signalbox at Taplow pictured here on 20 March 1962. This box, which was fitted with a 71-lever frame, was opened on 30 June 1930. It was converted to a 24-lever ground frame on 8 December 1963. Notice the lower windows, an unusual feature to survive as many of these boxes were bricked up during World War 2. *Great Western Trust*

was finally removed on 15 October 1933.

During 1932 passenger lines between Paddington and Southall West Junction were equipped with colour-light signalling. These signals were not of the multi-aspect type but were known as 'searchlights'. They replaced the existing mechanical signals and gave the same GW aspects of red and green for stop signals and yellow and green for distant. The Engine and Carriage Line signals were three aspect: green for clear; yellow for caution; and red for stop. At Paddington extensive alterations were made to the track layout to incorporate longer platforms and the enlargement of the Bishop's Road station. The signalling scheme saw the replacement of four old mechanical signalboxes with three new power-operated boxes. The first of these, at Westbourne Bridge, was brought into use on 10 January 1932. The new box contained 38 levers and replaced the old Westbourne Bridge box. Paddington Departure box contained 96 levers and was opened on 2 July 1933 and on 13 August 1933 the new Arrival box was opened. This latter box replaced those at Bishop's Road and Royal Oak. It was the largest of the three and contained a 184-lever frame. Power for the new installation was supplied by the GW's own sub-station at Royal Oak.

At 2am on the morning of 25 November 1938 fire broke out in the electric locking frame of the arrival signalbox at Paddington. Unfortunately, the signalmen on duty could not contain the blaze and the box was burnt out. The box controlled all the signalling and points on the arrival side of Paddington and also the Hammersmith & City lines between Paddington and Westbourne Park. Hand signalling had to be used until 18 December after which date temporary ground-frames were brought into use. Matters were made even worse when, on 23 December 1938, a second but less serious fire occurred at the Westbourne Bridge box. This was not so severely damaged and was reopened for use during February. The arrival box however was extensively damaged and was subsequently rebuilt and fitted with a new all-electric frame in July 1939.

In 1955 a decision was made to renew the signalling between Paddington and Southall. The railway was obviously short of money in those days, since it was decided to use as much of the existing equipment as possible because of the cost. The old searchlight signals were replaced by multiple-aspect types, but much of the old searchlight equipment was modified and reused. At West Ealing the signalbox was rebuilt with a new 71-lever frame. It was reopened on 20 March 1955 and replaced boxes at Hanwell, Drayton Green, Longfield Avenue and Ealing Broadway.

Left:
Ex-Great Western 2-6-2T No 6117 runs past Slough West box on 10 October 1963. Slough West was the largest of the three boxes at Slough. Opened in 1901 it was fitted with a 95-lever frame. Notice the bricked up windows. It was closed, together with Slough Middle and East boxes, with the opening of the new power box here on 14 June 1963. *R. C. Riley*

Right:
A pair of Type 3 (later Class 37) diesels Nos D6881/D6882 arrive at Paddington on 4 June 1965 with a special test train of 'XP64' stock and passing, on the right, the Paddington Arrival signalbox. This brick-built box contained a 184-lever frame and was opened on 2 July 1939. It replaced an earlier box which was opened on 13 August 1933 but had been subsequently destroyed by fire on 13 December 1938. *Ian Allan Library*

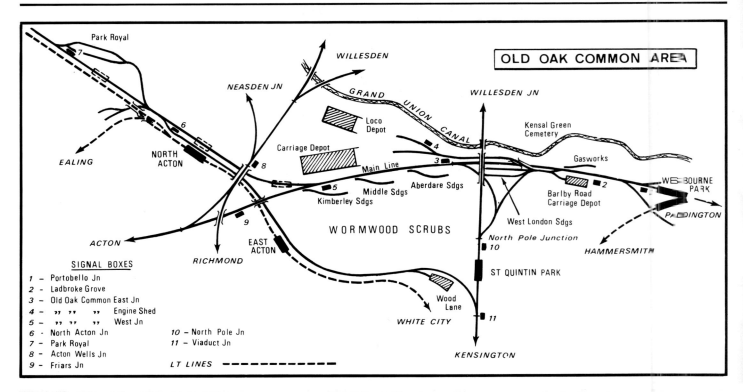

As part of the Western Region's modernisation plan a new power signalbox was opened at Old Oak Common on 8 October 1962. The new box, which was fitted with an entrance-exit route setting 'mosaic' type control panel, controlled the main, relief, and carriage lines over an area of approximately two to four miles from the terminus and replaced boxes at Old Oak East, Old Oak West and Friars Junction.

During 1962 a start was made on a £1½ million scheme for the complete

Above:
The new panel box at Old Oak Common pictured here on 27 September 1962. It was opened on 8 October 1962 and replaced a number of manual boxes in the area. *Ian Allan Library*

Right:
The interior of the panel box at Old Oak Common on 23 August 1962. *Ian Allan Library*

The interior of the panel box at Slough seen here on the opening day, 14 October 1963, with duty signalmen W. Northway and A. Moore. Slough was the second box to open under the Western Region's MAS scheme in the Thames Valley area. *Ian Allan Library*

resignalling of the 25-mile section between Hayes and Reading. The various alterations over the years had left a hotchpotch of signalling, with the section between Hayes and Langley controlled by a combination of colour-light and semaphore, that between Langley and Maidenhead by semaphores, and that from Maidenhead to Reading by colour-light. This latter section was completed on 23 October 1961 with the 10-mile section placed under the control of 'mosaic'-type control panels at Reading Main Line East and Twyford. The new system replaced eight mechanical boxes. The new box at Twyford contained a desk top control panel and a 56-level mechanical locking frame.

Work on the remaining section was completed when on 13 October 1963 a new power signalbox was opened at Slough. This box initially controlled the main line between Taplow and West Drayton and also the Windsor branch. The existing mechanical signalling at Maidenhead and West Drayton boxes continued to be used until 8 December 1963 when they were brought under the

control of Slough. The whole section was fitted with three and four aspect multi-lens colour-light signals, electric points and position-light ground signals for shunting.

A further phase in signalling modernisation was completed when a new power box was opened at Reading on 26 April 1965. The new box controlled 42 route miles and replaced 42 manual boxes. On 20 March 1972 its control was extended to take over the work of the remaining manual boxes at Twyford and Henley.

In 1965 the Western Region announced a £2 million modernisation programme for track remodelling and resignalling work on the approaches to Paddington. The work had to be completed in various stages because of traffic requirements. It was started on 15 October 1967 and was not finally completed until 13 May 1968. The newly remodelled trackwork and signalling now allowed two-way working in and out of all platforms at Paddington. All connections between the Western Region and Metropolitan line tracks

were removed. On 4 September 1967 the newly enlarged Old Oak panel box was opened and gradually took over control of all signal and train movements from the remaining mechanical boxes in the area. In anticipation of the introduction of High Speed Train services, which started on 4 October 1976, all the main line signalling was revised, with the introduction of longer sections, to allow for the higher speeds.

During 1989 a start was made on a £12 million resignalling scheme for the Chiltern line between Marylebone, Aylesbury and Banbury. Part of that work comprised the complete replacement of all the remaining mechanical boxes and signals on the old GW/GC section between Northolt and Princes Risborough. The work was finally completed on 10 August 1990 and today the line is under the control of the new Integrated Electronic Control Centre at Marylebone.

In 1992 work commenced on the complete resignalling of the main line between Paddington and Acton to give six bi-directional running lines into the terminus.

Under this scheme the power boxes at Old Oak Common and Slough have been replaced by a new IEC Centre at Slough. Eventually it is planned for the whole of the GW route between Paddington and Bristol to be controlled from one 'Super IEC Centre' at Swindon.

The new power box extension at Old Oak Common pictured here on 29 November 1966. Today this box is situated almost within the North Pole servicing complex and under the new IECC resignalling scheme will be closed and removed. *Ian Allan Library*

12. Locomotive Depots

During the early days of the Great Western, temporary engine sheds were established as and when the line was extended westwards. The first of these temporary sheds was erected at Drayton in around June 1837 in preparation for the first two engines — *Premier* and *Vulcan*. Daniel Gooch, who had set up his headquarters here in August 1837, supervised their delivery by canal on 10 November 1837. Of the two, *Vulcan* was the first to be steamed on 28 December. The only descriptive reference of the shed states that it was a single-road shed about one mile distant from the station. It was constructed of wood and capable of holding just two engines. The shed appears to have been in use during the construction of the line between 1837 and 1838.

Another temporary shed was constructed at Maidenhead (Taplow) in April 1838. Again information is sketchy but, as with Drayton, it was a single-road shed constructed in wood and capable of holding two engines. Reports state that the first engine to use the shed was *North Star*. This engine had been delivered to Maidenhead by barge in November 1837 and, although it was test steamed on 15 January 1838, it was not until 1 May that track laying had progressed sufficiently for it to reach the shed. Knowing the GW's reputation for the re-use of resources it is not beyond the realms of possibility that this could well have been a recycled 'Drayton'. The shed at Maidenhead was closed when the line was opened through to Reading in March 1840 but, according to a report by Gooch, was apparently still in situ, although unused, on 1 May 1841.

Temporary watering and coaling facilities were also provided at Twyford between 1839 and 1840 but there is no evidence to suggest a shed was ever provided here.

Paddington 1838-1852

This was the first large locomotive depot to be constructed by the Great Western Railway. Apart from the odd out-station it housed all the motive power available for the opening of the line.

This old lithograph shows the interior of the first engine shed at Paddington and is probably dated c1852. The two identifiable engines are *Elephant*, a 'Leo' class 2-2-2 built in 1841, and *Rover*, an 'Iron Duke' class 4-2-2 built in 1850. *G. Measom / Great Western Trust*

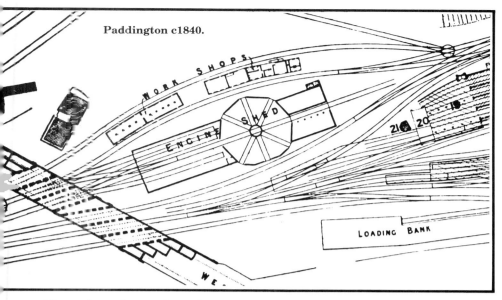

Paddington c1840.

The first locomotive depot at Paddington was constructed in around March or May 1838 and was certainly open for the commencement of passenger services on 4 June. The design of this first broad gauge 'engine house' was rather unusual as it comprised a central 130ft diameter roundhouse with a pair of straight sheds tagged on at each end. The whole complex, which was constructed of wood with a gable style roof measured about 360ft x 80ft, so it was quite a large building. It was situated in the yard just to the west of the original Paddington station and adjacent to Westbourne Terrace. The roundhouse contained a 35ft turntable and eight radial roads. The four-road straight shed at the west end measured 150ft x 30ft, and at the eastern end there was a single road repair depot. Early references to the shed seem to

suggest that the two straight sheds were constructed some time after the roundhouse and this is borne out by the fact that a second 35ft turntable was constructed around June 1841 in the adjacent loco yard to the west of Westbourne Terrace. This was probably to

One of the most elegant of Great Western designs was the Armstrong class 4-4-0s built in 1894. Here No 16 *Brunel*, in original condition, receives attention as it stands on the turntable road at Westbourne Park probably around the turn of the century. No 16 was rebuilt in September 1901 with a 'BRO'-type boiler. In April 1915 it was rebuilt once again and renamed and numbered 4169 *Charles Saunders*; it was withdrawn in July 1930. *Great Western Trust*

alleviate the congestion caused by the construction of the roundhouse extensions.

The engine shed was closed and removed in March 1852 to allow for the construction of the new Paddington station and during the same month a new and larger depot was opened at nearby Westbourne Park.

In steam two weeks ending 27 July 1850:
'Iron Duke' class 4-2-2:
Courier, Great Britain, Lightning, Pasha, Perseus, Prometheus, Sultan, Swallow, Tartar, Timour, Tornado, Wizard.
'Firefly' class 2-2-2:
Harpy, Hydra, Phlegethon, Phoenix, Pluto.

Westbourne Park 1852-1906

The GW was nothing if not consistent in moving loco depots from one cramped area at Paddington to another at nearby Westbourne Park. This quite large depot was opened officially on 2 March 1852 although it is quite possible that it was in use for several months prior to this date. For the new shed the roundhouse principle was abandoned, almost certainly due to the lack of space, and instead a 663ft-long straight shed was provided. It contained four roads and was constructed in brick with a gable-style slate roof so it was rather more substantial than the old Paddington shed. It had a maximum width of 63½ft. Just behind the shed was a 110ft x 53ft repair shop again built of brick. A 200ft-long coaling stage was situated partially under the Green Lane road bridge to the west of the shed building. This was operated using the crane and swing

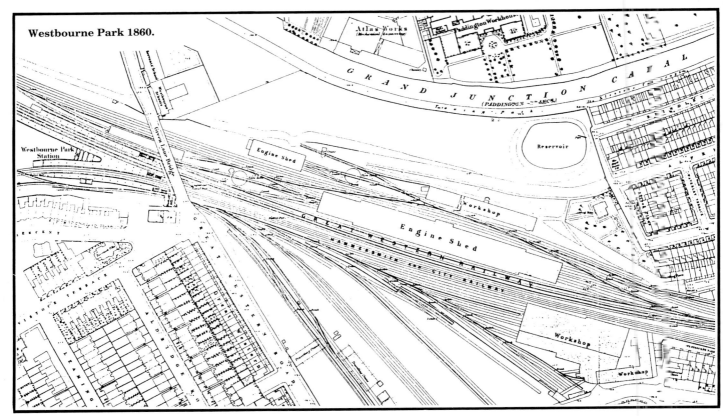

Westbourne Park 1860.

tub principle. An unusual feature of the coaling stage was that it was surmounted by a large clock tower which contained a four dial turret-type clock. A 45ft steam-operated turntable (possibly the only one in the country at the time) stood between the coaling plant and the shed. A second, hand-operated, 45ft turntable was added to the complex in around 1862. Both turntables were replaced with 55ft examples, in 1883 and 1895.

The workshops, stores and offices were also erected in 1852 and stood adjacent to the broad gauge shed. Interestingly the superintendent's office here was occupied for a time by Daniel Gooch until he moved to the general offices at the new Paddington station. During 1861/2 a separate three-road shed for

standard gauge engines was constructed. This new shed initially measured approximately 150ft x 45ft but, in 1873, it was widened to 90ft (six roads) in order to accommodate the increasing influx of standard gauge locomotives. Mixed gauge tracks had been gradually introduced into the old broad gauge shed from c1869.

Class 157 2-2-2 No 160 pictured here at Westbourne Park in c1880. No 160 was built at Swindon in December 1879 and, by the time it was withdrawn in September 1905, it had amassed 1,228,000 miles in service, which, incidentally, was the highest of the class. Notice also the mixed gauge track in the foreground. *Ian Allan Library*

The construction of new relief lines into Paddington required the removal of the coaling stage to a new position west of the Green Lane bridge and adjacent to Westbourne Park station. Again, lack of space saw the coaling stage shortened to 150ft.

Other buildings on site included a separate lifting shop and some repair shops. The broad gauge tracks were removed from the mixed gauge shed after the end of the broad gauge on 20 May 1892.

This was a large and busy depot and, by 1901, it had an allocation of some 136 engines. The confined space together with the long shed must have made working and servicing very difficult. It was probably this problem that stirred the GW into constructing a

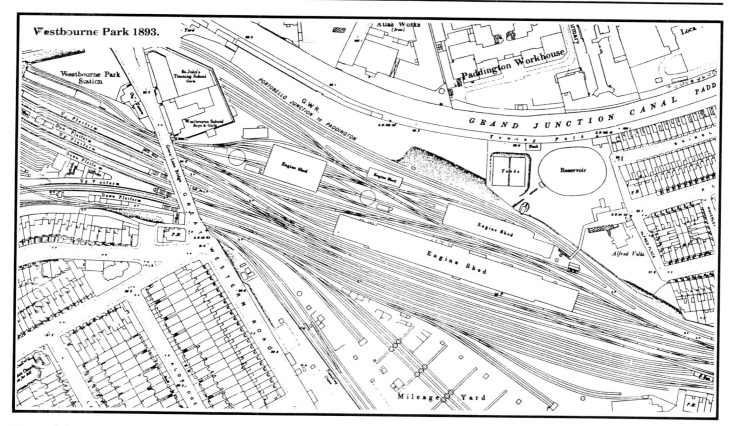

Westbourne Park 1893.

This general view shows the former broad gauge shed at Westbourne Park. The shed was opened in 1852 and was closed when the new shed at Old Oak Common was opened in 1906. The sign above the second road reads 'BG 2'. *L&GRP*

Dean '455' 'Metropolitan' class 2-4-0 No 1404 pictured at Westbourne Park in c1880. The engine was built in June 1878 and is fitted with condensing apparatus for working over the Metropolitan lines. In January 1901 it was fitted with larger 1,080gal water tanks, again for Metropolitan working. It was withdrawn from traffic in February 1934. *Ian Allan Library*

new depot on a large area of land approximately three miles west of Paddington and adjacent to the Paddington branch of the Grand Junction Canal. Westbourne Park was officially closed on 18 March 1906 and was demolished soon afterwards. It is interesting to note that up until the end of operations at this depot the two buildings were still known as the 'standard' and 'broad gauge' sheds, even though the latter had not seen a broad gauge engine for some 14 years.

Broad Gauge Allocation. In steam 19 days ending 19 July 1862.
Passenger engines:
Iron Duke' Class 4-2-2:
Balaclava, Emperor, Estaffete, Eupatoria, Great Britain, Hirondelle, Lightning, Perseus,

Rover, Tartar, Timour, Warlock, Wizard
Metropolitan 2-4-0T: *Bey*
'Star' class 2-2-2: *Evening Star*
'Great Western' class 4-2-2: *Great Western*
'Waverley' class 4-4-0: *Lalla Rookh*
Goods Engines:
Gooch Standard Goods 0-6-0:
Banshee, Boyne, Brutus, Clyde, Coquette, Diana, Giaour, Gyfeillon, Hades, Janus, Mersey, Metis, Midas, Minerva, Neptune, Octavia, Orson, Sphinx, Tweed, Ulysses, Vixen, Warhawk, Wye, Severn
'Leo' class 2-4-0: *Dromedary, Libra, Stromboli*
'Caesar' class 0-6-0: *Hero*

Early sub sheds

Hammersmith 1864-1907 (Sub to Westbourne Park)

This two-road depot was built by the GWR & Metropolitan Joint Railway in June 1864. The shed which measured 115½ft x 29ft was constructed of brick with a gable-style timber roof. Although the shed remained open until the electrification of the line on 1 January 1907 allocations of GW engines had ceased in 1905. The shed was used during this latter period for stabling Metropolitan engines.

Standard Gauge Allocation as at 1 January 1901:

'Metro' class 2-4-0T: 1404, 1406, 1408, 1416, 3583, 3594

Farringdon Street 1863-1865

(This shed for a short time was also a sub shed to Westbourne Park.)
According to the records a single-road shed was opened here by the Great Western & Metropolitan Joint Railway on 10 January 1863. The shed was constructed of wood and measured 110ft x 20ft. Entrance was effected via a 45ft turntable. The shed fell out of use after the opening of Hammersmith and was demolished in December 1865 when the line was extended through to Moorgate. No allocation details survive.

It appears that for a few months at least during 1905 locomotives were also stabled at Bishop's Road station. The following piece is taken from the GW magazine of that date and mentions the change over from steam to electric traction: 'provision has been made at Bishop's Road for changing engines which will be used in connection with certain of the Hammersmith trains, nine of which are daily being worked electrically between Bishop's Road and Aldgate'.

Paddington: Old Oak Common 1906-1993

Westbourne Park was replaced by the new engine shed at Old Oak Common. The shed, designed by G. J. Churchward and built by Walkerdines of Derby, took almost four years to complete and was opened on 17 March 1906. This vast building, which covered a total area of some 215,000sq ft, was the largest engine shed on the GW and certainly the most spectacular in the country at the time. The main building

measured 444ft x 360ft and was constructed of red Staffordshire brick. The roof section was slated and glazed in 60ft bays and supported using pitched pine principals with steel tie rods. These were supported by steel girders which in turn were supported on cast-iron columns.

Housed within its walls were four 65ft undergirder Ransomes and Rapier electrically-operated turntables, each having 28 radial roads and giving accommodation for up to 112 locomotives. A separate 12-road repair shop was provided alongside the main building, and each road contained a 52ft pit. This building was constructed of brick like the shed, and measured 195ft x 101ft. The fitters and machine shop measured 195ft x 45 ft and contained a 30-ton electrically-driven overhead travelling crane. Entrance to the repair shop was via an electrically-operated traverser. Other buildings included smiths', coppersmiths' and carpenters' shops as well as a large block housing the stores and foreman's office.

Everything about the new depot was on the grand scale including locomotive servicing facilities. The double-sided coaling plant measuring 104 x 59ft and contained four double and two single tips. Over this, and supported on a brick base, stood the shed water tank, whose four sections held 290,000 gal of water. In 1934 the GW undertook a series of improvements to the depot with the provision of new buildings for offices and messrooms. During World War 2 a new staff canteen was constructed and in 1942 the ash roads were covered by a large corrugated iron shed. In 1947, and in anticipation of the short

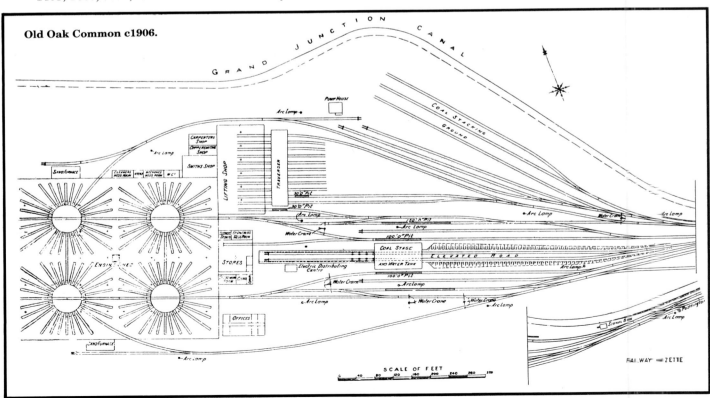

Old Oak Common c1906.

The interior of one of the roundhouses at Old Oak pictured here during construction in, probably, c1905. Notice the office in the centre of the picture. *Great Western Trust*

A similar picture, but taken in 1911 some five years after opening, shows a wide variety of engines. Notice the mixture of gas and electric lighting above the turntable and also that each smoke vent is individually numbered. *Great Western Trust*

'633' class 0-6-0 condensing tank No 643 and 'County' class 4-4-0 No 3807 *County Kilkenny* stand outside the repair shop at Old Oak Common in 1932. *Great Western Trust*

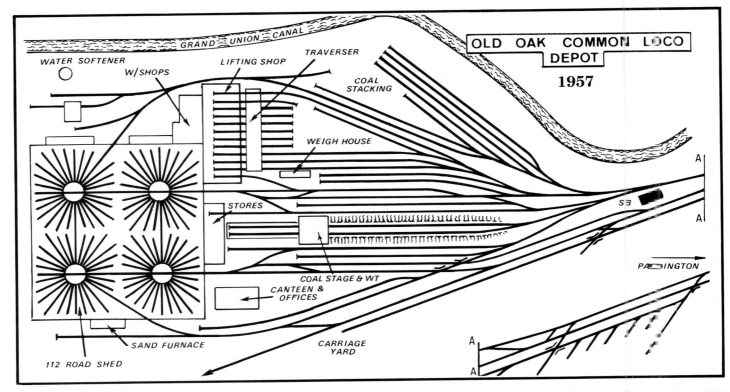

OLD OAK COMMON LOCO DEPOT
1957

GRAND UNION CANAL

WATER SOFTENER
W/SHOPS
LIFTING SHOP
TRAVERSER
COAL STACKING
WEIGH HOUSE
STORES
COAL STAGE & WT
CANTEEN & OFFICES
SAND FURNACE
112 ROAD SHED
CARRIAGE YARD
PADDINGTON
SB

GWR 350hp 0-6-0 diesel-electric shunter No 2 renumbered as BR No 15100 at Old Oak Common in the summer of 1948. The engine was built by Hawthorn Leslie and purchased by the GWR in April 1936. It worked for a number of years at Acton, but was later moved to Bristol from were it was withdrawn in July 1965. *A. A. Delicata*

One of the features of Old Oak was the large number of express passenger engines stabled around the turntable roads. This is well demonstrated in this picture taken on 8 May 1960 of Nos 7001 *Sir James Milne*, 5042 *Winchester Castle*, 6021 *King Richard II*, 5072 *Hurricane* and 4087 *Cardigan Castle*. By this date a number of the roof smoke extractors seem have been removed. *A. A. Delicata*

This interesting picture shows the ash discharging shutes at Old Oak. These were apparently operated by steam as the engine steam pipe is connected to the machine. *Ian Allan Library*

lived oil-burning experiment, a pair of 175,000 gal oil tanks were installed adjacent to the repair shop. The pumping plant, which was steam heated, was capable of pumping up to 20,000 gal per hour from rail tankers into the main tanks and then to locomotives.

During the 1950s the depot saw little change but under the Western Region modernisation plan, Old Oak was designated one of the six major diesel servicing and maintenance depots to be provided on the Region.

The introduction of diesel-hydraulic locomotives onto Western Region passenger services during the late 1950s and early 1960s saw the steam allocation at Old Oak Common plummet and during the autumn of 1963 a start was made in converting Old Oak into a diesel depot. The main shed building was demolished during March 1964 and in January 1965 a new three-road single-storey diesel servicing shed was brought into use. This was erected over the site of the old southern bay turntable and contained room for up to six locomotives. Interestingly, one of the 175,000 gal tanks that was erected in 1947 was still in situ, and was retained as the main fuel oil store.

Old Oak was not officially closed to steam until 22 March 1965, when its few remaining serviceable engines moved down the line to Southall. Only the western bay turntable of the old steam depot was retained as a diesel stabling area. However, the old steam repair shop was converted into a seven-bay heavy maintenance factory. The new depot, which was officially opened on 20 October 1965, cost £500,000 and provided full maintenance facilities for up to 70 main line and 25 shunting locomotives, with daily servicing for another 65.

Today Old Oak Common is the main servicing depot for Network SouthEast, InterCity, Parcels, Red Star and Engineering section Class 47 locomotives, although other types also use the facilities. With the introduction of new Turbo Units on Thames Line and Waterloo-Exeter services the locomotive allocation at Old Oak has dropped considerably. The depot was essentially divided into two parts — fuel/servicing and heavy maintenance — but, in March 1993, the heavy maintenance factory was closed. However, servicing and 'A' examination facilities are being retained.

'87xx' class 0-6-0 condensing tank No 9700 is pictured at Old Oak Common on 16 August 1959. This engine was constructed as No 8700 in 1931 and was converted into a condensing tank in March 1932. In January 1934 it was incorporated into the new batch of condensing tanks and renumbered 9700. *Dr John Coiley*

A view of the turntable area at Old Oak Common on 28 April 1988 shows Class 47 Nos 47500 *Great Western* (in GW green) and 47450. Also visible is Class 50 No 50023 *Howe*. *Brian Morrison*

Old Oak Common HST and DMU Depot

High Speed trains were introduced on to Western Region services on 4 October 1976 and, at the same time, a purpose-built maintenance facility was constructed at Old Oak over part of the carriage sidings. The new shed, which contained three roads, was initially constructed to service up to two seven-car HST sets at a time. In 1985 the accommodation at this shed was extended to enable longer HST formations, and the displaced DMU sets from Southall, to be serviced. Some DMU and HST maintenance is also undertaken in the adjacent 15-road carriage shed, although this is mainly used for stabling purposes. As mentioned above, with the introduction of Turbos (which are serviced at Reading) on to Thames line services, and the gradual replacement of the 'heritage' DMU sets, there must obviously be a question-mark over the long-term viability of this servicing facility.

Right:
The interior of the factory at Old Oak on 16 April 1932 contains a collection of tank and tender engines under repair.
E. R. Wethersett

Below:
The factory some 50 years later, on 1 February 1982, shows HST powercar No 43133 under repair. *Brian Morrison*

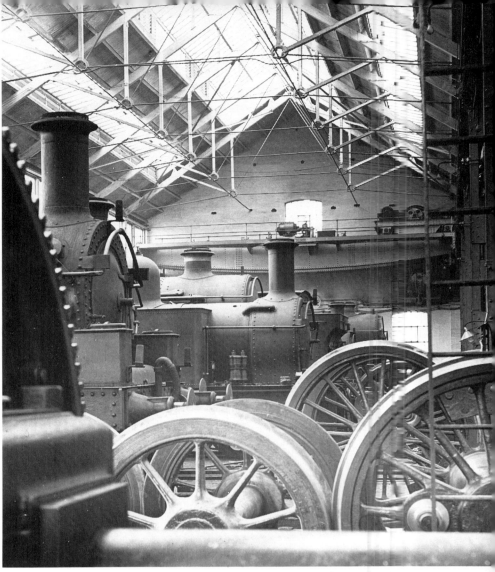

Ranelagh Bridge 1907-1980

The small depot at Ranelagh Bridge was opened on 27 June 1907. It was not a sub shed as such, but was constructed to provide watering and turning facilities for engines that were booked for a quick turn round at Paddington and did not require a longer service at Old Oak Common. The yard, which was adjacent to the old GW offices at Porchester Road, was provided with a 65ft turntable and a 22,500 gal water tank. Surprisingly, no coaling facilities were provided here. The depot had accommodation for about 15 engines and at the height of operations could service 65-80 engines each weekday. The general turn around time was about 65min. The end of steam traction out of Paddington saw the turntable removed and, in April 1964, the yard was converted to a diesel stabling point, much to the annoyance of the dwellers in the nearby terraced houses, who, instead of having to put up with a certain amount of smoke, now had to put up with noisy and smelly diesels. The rundown of Ranelagh started with the introduction of the first HSTs in October 1976, and by the summer of 1979 when HSTs had taken over most of the long-distance services, the depot became surplus to requirements. It was finally closed in 1980. For a number of years the yard lay derelict but during September 1990 Ranelagh Bridge yard was converted into a car park.

Slough 1840-1868

This single-road broad gauge shed was opened in around November 1840 and stood to the west of Slough station. Entrance to the shed was through a separate arch under the nearby road bridge. A 25ft turntable was situated between the shed and the bridge. The

Top left:
This fine study shows Wolverhampton (Stafford Road)-allocated 'King' No 6008 *King James II* being turned at Ranelagh Bridge in c1949. *John Ashman*

Centre left:
An excellent view of Ranelagh Bridge yard taken on 6 August 1960. It was not much fun for the inhabitants of the adjacent houses — notice the washing hanging out to dry! Locomotive interest from left to right: Nos 1027 *County of Stafford*, 70025 *Western Star*, 7003 *Elmley Castle*, 7020 *Gloucester Castle*, 5044 *Earl of Dunraven* and 6011 *King James I*. *R. C. Riley*

Left:
After the withdrawal of steam traction Ranelagh continued to be used as a diesel stabling point. Awaiting their next turn of duty on 21 May 1975 are Nos 50046 *Ajax*, 47477, 47272 and 47068. The introduction of HSTs saw the role of Ranelagh diminish and it was closed during 1980. *Brian Morrison*

building itself measured 135x 18ft and, although there was room for up to three engines, generally at this time only two worked from here. Early plans for the Windsor branch show the east curve of the new branch actually running through the shed! However, when the branch was constructed in 1849, the course was altered slightly and the shed survived. It was eventually closed in 1868, although by this time it must have been in a poor state, as its dilapidated condition had been mentioned in company minutes in both 1863 and 1865.

Broad Gauge Allocation:

In steam
27 July 1850, unclassified 2-2-2:
Snake, Viper
19 July 1862, 'Sun' class 2-2-2:
Assagais, Djerid, Eclipse, Rocket
'Metropolitan' Class 2-4-0T: *Shah*

Slough 1868-1964

The 1865 company minutes relating to the condition of the broad gauge shed also contained reference to an estimate of £1,800 'to provide a new shed at Slough to accommodate up to 6 engines'. This replacement, of which early details are sketchy, apparently came into use during 1868 and was, according to the records, converted from a goods shed. Whether this is the case or not, the

In 1954 the shed was modernised with a new roof and brick end gables, as can be seen in this picture taken in 1959. Interestingly, even the small lean-to shed, which was erected as a temporary measure, has also been reclad.
Lens of Sutton

'new' engine shed was situated south of the Windsor branch line to the west of Slough station. It was constructed of brick with a slated roof and contained two roads. One terminated inside the building, and the other ran at a slight angle through the shed and to a small coal stage. In 1872 the shed was enlarged to four roads by the addition of a second building, and the enlarged shed then measured 135ft x 65ft. During 1885 the old coal stage was removed and replaced with a standard GWR pattern. It measured 40ft x 23ft, and was

A view of the locoyard at Slough in Great Western days. The allocation here comprised mainly 0-6-0PTs and 2-6-2Ts, a number of which can be seen in this photograph. The corrugated iron lean-to was constructed in c1935 to provide a fifth covered road. *Lens of Sutton*

built of brick, and supported a 45,000 gal water tank. Also around this time a 45ft turntable was installed on the site of the old broad gauge shed. Around 1935 a 135ft x 15ft corrugated iron lean-to was added to the side of the old building giving a fifth covered road. In 1954 the shed was provided with a new roof, and the old slates were replaced by asbestos sheeting. At the same time the timber gables at each end of the shed were replaced by brick and new wooden smoke extractors were fitted. Throughout its life the allocation here comprised mainly tank engines, which were used for local duties (including the Windsor, Marlow and Watlington branches). The shed closed on 1 June 1964 and the remaining locomotives were transferred to nearby Southall. The shed stood unused for a number of years but was demolished in May 1970. Today the site is used as a car park.

Marlow 1872-1962 (Sub shed to Slough)

This small brick-built shed measured 22ft x 50ft and was opened by the Great Marlow Railway in 1872. The shed was served by a single siding along which stood a small coaling stage and a 13,000 gal water tank. The shed was closed to steam in July 1962 but was not demolished until June 1964.

Southall (Brentford Branch) 1859-84

This small single-road broad gauge shed was opened by the Great Western & Brentford Railway on 18 July 1859. The Gooch registers list the shed as 'Brentford Branch' and not Southall. The building, which was probably constructed of brick with a gabled roof, measured 75ft x 15ft. Entrance to the shed was via a 40ft turntable. The shed

was situated to the east of Southall station and adjacent to the Brentford branch junction. The shed was closed and demolished in June 1884.

Allocations:

In steam for opening of the line on 18 July 1859:
'Fury' class 0-6-0: *Hercules*
In steam two weeks ending 19 July 1862:
'Sun' class 2-2-2: *Antelope*
'Star' class 2-2-2: *North Star*
Gooch Standard Goods 0-6-0: *Wellington*

Southall 1884-1986

By the 1880s it was obvious to the GW that the old Brentford Branch shed at Southall was completely inadequate for the amount of traffic being generated in the area and, in July 1883, plans were made for the construction of a brand

new engine shed. The new shed, which was built on the same site, opened in June 1884 and measured 100ft x 100ft. It contained six roads and was built in brick with a wooden north-light pattern glazed and slated roof. A single-road repair shop and offices, also built in brick, ran alongside the northern wall. Behind the shed stood a 45ft turntable, which was replaced in March 1909 with a larger 65ft table. A separate 200ft x 20ft corrugated iron railmotor shed,

This view shows the large steam depot at Southall probably in c1957. The original shed here was opened in 1884 and was partially demolished in 1954 to make way for the new shed pictured here. As can be seen the shed was situated between the main line on the left and the Brentford branch on the right. *British Rail*

which stood to the south of Brentford branch, was opened on 28 September 1904. The shed coaling plant was a standard GW single-sided pattern over which stood a 43,000 gal water tank. In 1953 the Western Region completely rebuilt the shed, demolishing much of the old depot. The new steam shed which finally opened in 1954 still contained six roads, but an additional two-road, 275ft x 100ft, diesel depot was constructed on the site of the old repair shop. The main building was steel-framed on a brick base and measured 210ft x 100ft. The whole complex was covered with a corrugated and glazed roof. Ventilation was via a series of large Robertson roof vents. A new, and separate, 120ft x 35ft brick-built repair shop with roller shutter-type doors was constructed in the yard to the east of the shed building. To allow for the expansion of the shed the 65ft turntable was also moved to a new position further east. The old coaling plant was abandoned although the water tank continued in use but, unusually, the new coaling plant used the rather old-fashioned tub-and-hoist system. Throughout its life the majority of Southall's allocation was for goods work but, in the early 1960s, part of the shed was given over to the servicing of the newly-introduced Thames Valley DMU fleet. Steam continued at the depot and the closure to steam of Old Oak Common and Slough in 1964 saw Southall become a dumping ground for redun-

dant steam engines. It was not to be long before the creeping malaise reached Southall and, in September 1965, the shed lost its allocation of steam locomotives, although it continued to be used for servicing purposes until it was finally closed to steam traction on 31 December 1965. The shed was soon converted into a full DMU depot, and amongst the various alterations undertaken was the provision of a large fuel bay. An unusual feature of the diesel era was the replacement of the old steam turntable with a small triangle of lines, installed to allow turning of DMU sets. The diesel depot finally closed in November 1986, and its work was taken over by Reading and a new depot at Old Oak Common. At the time of writing the shed still stands and is occupied by a preservation group. The old repair shop at the back of the shed has been used for the last few years to stable steam locos working on specials in the London area.

Uxbridge 1856-97

Uxbridge shed was opened by the GW on 8 September 1856. It stood adjacent to the station and was constructed of brick with a gable-style slate roof and measured about 90ft x 20ft. Next to the shed was a small water tank under which stood the shed coaling plant, and a 25ft diameter turntable stood nearby. The line, together with the engine shed, was converted from broad to standard gauge during 5-9 October 1871. The shed was closed in December 1897 when locomotive workings were taken over by Southall. The building stood for a while after closure but was eventually demolished in November 1899. The Uxbridge branch, which was the very first GW branch to be constructed in London, closed to passenger services on 8 September 1962.

Allocation:

In steam for opening of line on 8th September 1856:
Unclassified 2-2-2: Vulcan.
In steam for two weeks ending 19 July 1862:
Unclassified 2-2-2: Apollo.

Staines 1885-1952

This small single-road shed was opened by the Staines & West Drayton Railway on 2 November 1885. It was taken over by the Great Western Railway in 1900. The shed was constructed of timber with a slated roof and measured approximately 40ft x 20ft. The shed normally housed one or two small tank locomotives that were used on the branch but, during the early 1950s, ex-GW diesel railcars took over many of the branch services and the shed was closed in June 1952.

Allocations:

1 January 1901:
'455' class 'Metro' 2-4-0T: 616
1 January 1930:
'517' class 0-4-2T: 575

Henley On Thames (Sub shed to Reading) 1857-1958

This single-road broad gauge shed was opened in June 1857. It measured 58ft 6in x 20ft, and was constructed of brick with a slated roof. Inside was a 44ft 8in pit. The shed was converted from broad to standard gauge on 24 March 1876. In c1904 the shed was extended to give an overall length of about 80ft and around the same time the old 45ft turntable was replaced by a 55ft example. The shed water tank (6,500 gal) was situated above an unusual brick-built coaling platform, which fell out of use

c1897. With the removal of steam traction from branch services, the shed was closed on 5 October 1958. Today the site is covered by housing.

Allocations:

In steam for the opening of the line 1 June 1857:
'Leo' class 2-4-0T: *Virgo*
In steam 2 weeks ending 19 July 1862
Unclassified 2-2-2: *Eagle, Vulcan*
'Firefly' 2-2-2: *Lynx*
1 January 1901:
'517' class 0-4-2T: 1482
1 January 1920:
'517' class 0-4-2T: 1485

Although just out of the scope of this book I have included Wycombe for, at one time, it was the terminus of the branch from Maidenhead.

Wycombe (Wycombe Railway) 1854-70

This small single-road depot was opened by the Wycombe Railway on 1 August 1854. The shed measured 45ft x 25ft and was probably constructed of wood. It stood alongside the original terminus station at Wycombe, and was provided with a 20ft-diameter turntable and coaling stack situated some distance away to the east.

The shed was closed in August 1870 and was subsequently converted, together with the old terminus station, into a goods shed.

Allocation at opening:

'Sun' class 2-2-2T: *Aurora, Javelin*

A note on Great Western Railway locomotive allocations used in this book.

Broad gauge engines were not listed by the GW as being allocated to any one depot. Instead they were shown as being 'in steam' at a particular location or 'station'. This information is contained in the *Gooch Registers of Engines in Steam* which lists the location of the engines on a two-weekly basis between 1850 and 1862.

From January 1901 proper locomotive allocation books were kept, which all survive and show again, on a two weekly basis, precisely where each locomotive was allocated. It is quite probable that written allocation records were kept prior to 1901 but, if this was the case, certainly to my knowledge, none of these appears to have survived.

A row of condemned 0-6-0PTs stands at the back of Southall shed on 8 August 1965. By this time the shed had officially lost its allocation of steam locomotives but it continued to be used as a stabling point until 31 December 1965 after which date Western Region steam was officially withdrawn. *R. C. Riley*

13. The Old Oak Common and West London Carriage Sidings

Before the opening of new carriage sidings at Old Oak Common in 1905, carriages were serviced at the West London Carriage Sidings which were situated on the south side of the line at Kensal Green. These sidings had been established in c1886 to replace the old carriage sidings that were situated at Paddington station. In his reminiscences F. W. Hatton, who was employed at Paddington during this time, relates that the first three trains to be stabled at the West London Sidings were West of England broad gauge services.

A small carriage repair depot was established at Paddington soon after the completion of the station in 1854. This building was constructed of wood. This continued to be used until the turn of the century, after which it was removed to allow for the construction of Platform No 1A. The West London Sidings dealt with both main line and suburban traffic and by c1904 had expanded to comprise 34 storage roads and four carriage sheds — three in the west yard and a large shed to the east at Barlby Road. There was also a small gasworks here, supplying gas for carriage lighting. By this date the West London sidings had become extremely

congested and, during 1905, a new carriage shed and sidings were opened at Old Oak. The new shed, which was 1,000ft long and 296ft wide contained four bays each with five roads of track. A 50ft turntable was provided in the centre of the main yard and was used for turning both carriages and locomotives. There were 12 reception and 41 stabling sidings.

When opened, the new depot was immediately put to use in servicing the main line coaching stock. The old depot at West London was, however, retained for suburban use.

The movement of locomotives and empty stock between Paddington, West London Junction and Old Oak Common was becoming an increasing problem. In order to alleviate the congestion between these points, the GW constructed a separate pair of running lines between Old Oak and Westbourne Park. These allowed locomotives and coaching stock to move between depot and station without obstructing the main running lines. The crossing from the north to the south side of the main line was accomplished with the construction of a 270ft long double track girder bridge, near the West London

Sidings. The bridge was reached via two inclines each a quarter of a mile in length. It was the original intention of the GW to construct a tunnel under the main line but, due to cost and the possibility of flooding, it was abandoned in favour of the bridge. Work on the whole project was started in August 1911 and was finished in November 1912.

With the introduction of new coaching stock and longer trains the marshalling of coaching stock at Old Oak became a problem with much 'double shunting' required. In order to alleviate the problem the company authorised, in 1935, an extension to the carriage shed, the rearrangement of the carriage sidings, and the provision of a carriage repair depot. The work was started during the following year and was not finished until April 1940.

It was also probably around this time that the layout at the West London sidings was rationalised with the removal of the southernmost carriage shed and the rearrangement of several of the sidings.

The first part of the work to be completed at Old Oak was the provision of 10 new carriage and van sidings to the north of the depot. These were brought into use during 1939 and were known as the 'Coronation sidings'. They increased the holding capacity of the depot by about 300 coaches and were used mainly for stabling coaching stock used for excursion and special trains.

The existing carriage shed was extended by a further two bays, 940ft long by 148ft wide, giving another 10 roads of covered accommodation. The enlarged shed now had 30 roads which

HST set No 253004 stands inside the HST servicing shed at Old Oak Common on 3 March 1985. The shed, which was constructed in 1976, was extended during 1985 to take the longer HST sets. *Colin J. Marsden*

The interior of the old Pullman shed at Old Oak on 8 February 1993. Today the shed is used for various activities including electrical repairs, painting and the repair of freightliner and other wagons. *Author*

gave storage accommodation for 420 coaches. Some idea of the size can be gleaned from the fact that the roof area covered some 439,310sq ft. Each road was provided with steam heating, the outlets being supplied from a new boiler house that was constructed adjacent to the shed.

The roof of the carriage shed consisted of Robertson's protected metal 'V'-beamed sheeting with four sections of glazing 8ft deep, running the whole length of each roof. To enable the glazing to be cleaned, each roof was fitted with a movable gangway.

In order to serve the new shed extension the depot reception and outgoing roads were rearranged. In the yard the old 50ft turntable was replaced by a new 70ft example and a 200ft platform was erected for the washing out of horseboxes.

Adjacent to the carriage shed was the carriage lifting, repair and paint shops. This large brick building was not fully opened for use until 1941. The main lifting shop was 412ft long and 70ft wide and contained electric hoists, wheel-turning lathes and various other machines. To lift the coaches from their bogies two 20-ton electrically-operated overhead travelling cranes were installed. These had a 67ft span and were able to traverse the whole length of the lifting shop. The paint shop contained three roads and was 592ft long and 70ft wide. It is interesting to note that during World War 2 these two shops housed Italian prisoners of war

Today part of the old Great Western carriage shed is used for stabling HST sets. In this picture taken on 8 February 1993 six sets can be seen. *Author*

who were serving out their time as railway navvies.

The large boiler house was fitted with three Lancashire boilers each fitted with mechanical stokers, and provided steam heating to 56 of the carriage roads. Old Oak Common was, in its time, the largest passenger marshalling yard in England, with some 10½ miles of sidings. At its peak, over 600 men were employed on the servicing, maintenance and preparation of carriages. The depot dealt with up to 2,000 passenger coaches each day, with trains booked to leave the depot for Paddington at five-minute intervals.

With a few minor alterations the carriage depots at Old Oak and West London remained pretty well intact well into the 1950s but, on 23 April 1959, a new layout was brought into use at the West London Depot. Two of the three carriage sheds in the west yard were removed, and the remaining shed was retained for carriage and wagon repairs. A two-road DMU servicing shed was erected in the northwest corner of the sidings. This shed remained in use until 7 November 1966 when DMU servicing was switched to Southall. The DMU shed was demolished shortly afterwards. On 20 November 1966 the carriage washing plant at West London was closed and a new plant was opened on the north side of the main line on the site of the old up and down goods lines. The end of steam traction, and the gen-

eral reduction in coaching stock and engine movements, saw the down side overbridge line at Kensal Green taken out of use on 4 September 1967. The remaining track is today signalled for two way working. The rationalisation at West London was finally completed on 30 June 1969 when the remains of the carriage sidings were finally removed.

During 1962 carriage servicing facilities at Old Oak were also rationalised with the reconstruction of the old carriage sheds. Covered accommodation was retained over roads 1-15 but was removed from 16 to 30, although the end walls and offices were retained.

In 1960 the old paint shops at Old Oak were converted into a servicing shed for the newly introduced 'Blue Pullman' diesel units. This facility was closed on 4 May 1973 when 'Pullman' services on the Western Region were withdrawn. Today the 'Pullman' shed is used for electrical and wagon repairs and also as a paint shop. The adjacent building is still retained as the heavy lift and wheel lathe shop.

In September 1976 a new three-road HST servicing shed was opened alongside the existing carriage shed on the site of the old field sidings. During 1986 this was extended to accommodate the newly-formed eight-car HST sets and the various DMUs that had been allocated to Old Oak after the closure of Southall. The enlarged shed was open for traffic on 11 May 1986.

14. Hayes Creosoting Depot

Hayes Creosoting Depot was situated approximately 11 miles from Paddington and on the south side of the line between Southall and Hayes. Prior to the opening of this depot the GW were storing sleepers and other timbers at their small yard at Chelsea Basin on the West London line. This soon proved to be inadequate and in 1875 a decision was made to construct a new yard and creosoting plant at Hayes.

This was opened on 6 June 1877 and covered an area of some 11 acres. It was situated adjacent to the Paddington Arm of the Grand Junction Canal, and prior to its opening the GW had widened the canal and constructed a small wharf. Rail access was via a single siding that ran from Hayes station and down the embankment into the yard. The new depot opened with the minimum of equipment. At first there was just one cylinder, a vacuum oil tank and some force pumps but eventually the yard was provided with a fully-equipped pressurised creosoting works with drying and pickling areas. Initially the work at Hayes was carried out by a 15-man team of contractors. Early reports show that about 80,000 pieces of timber were transported via special sleeper trains to the new depot from Chelsea and that, due to lack of equipment, the contractors had difficulty in both unloading and stacking it.

New timbers arrived via the canal and here difficulties in unloading persisted for a number of years until steam hoists were installed. Prior to this, sleepers were unloaded using rope pulleys and derricks, operated at first by hand but later by horse. Using this latter method was very hit and miss for if the horse failed to stop at the appropriate time the sleepers were pulled right through over the top of the derrick. In 1884 with the output running at about 2,000 sleepers per week the GW took over the operation of the yard from the contractor. They promptly installed steam hoists in the yard and the adja-

cent storage yard to deal with the unloading problems. This now allowed the timber to be stacked to a height of 40ft, thus allowing greater storage space. Each stack was served via a rail siding. The removal of the broad gauge saw the need for sleepers grow and, in 1894, further improvements were made by the addition of adzing, chairing and boring machines. Additional creosoting cylinders, storage tanks, force and vacuum pumps were added in 1895. These improvements to the plant saw sleeper production soar and, by 1911, the workforce had grown to 140 men turning out 11,000 sleepers per week. For many years the raw sleepers were cut from Baltic Pine and shipped in from the Baltic ports of Memel and Riga but, in

later years, Douglas Fir and Jarrah, imported from California and Australia were used. Once creosoted the sleepers had an expected service life of between 18 and 22 years.

During 1935 the works were once again enlarged and now covered an area of some 21 acres. Three five-ton capacity travelling cranes were installed alongside the canal wharf and a new stacking and holding yard was constructed. This now gave storage room for some ¾ million sleepers plus timber for crossings, etc. New 5-ton capacity electric hoists were installed in the yard and much of the old creosoting plant was replaced, as were the boring and adzing machines. The whole of of the new plant was now placed under cover. The two new creosoting cylinders, which measured 90ft x 6ft 9in, each held 600 sleepers and operated under a pressure of 200lb per sq in. The improvements gave the plant the capacity to deal with ½ million sleepers per year and for this the works was consuming some 1½ million gallons of creosote per year. Because of the large fire risk the whole yard was provided with hydrants which were supplied by two electrically operated fire pumps. By the late 1950s the use of continuously welded track and concrete sleepers saw the need for wooden sleepers diminish and gradually the works were run down finally closing in June 1964. Today the site is covered by a large rubbish incinerator.

I include this brief explanation of how the sleepers were made.

The raw timber was cut at source into 9ft x 10in x 10in lengths. On arrival in this country these were cut in half length ways, each piece thus giving two 9ft x 10in x 5in sleepers. After delivery to Hayes, the timber was inspected, stacked in 'avenues' and allowed to season for about six months. These avenues of sleepers could be up to 40ft high and several hundred yards in length. Once the seasoning had taken place the sleepers were then loaded on

Working notice. *Great Western Trust*

Charging one of the large creosote cylinders each cylinder held between 300 c 350 sleepers. The charging process took around three hours and consumed 3½ gal of creosote per sleeper. *Great Western Trust*

to specially constructed 'sleeper' trolleys. From here they were taken to the adzing and boring shed where they were fed individually through the various machines. The adzing, or plaining, machine ensured the sleepers were of uniform thickness, and the boring machine made the holes for the chairplates. When this had been completed the sleepers were moved to the creosot-ing cylinders, which could hold up to 600 sleepers at a time. Once loaded, the cylinder was hermetically sealed, and a vacuum pump was used to evacuate any air from the cylinder. Then the creosote oil, pre-heated to a temperature of about 120°F, was forced into the cylinder at a pressure of about 200lb/sq in. The impregnation process took about 1¼hr to complete, and in this time each sleeper absorbed some 3½ gal of creosote. From here the sleeper passed through to the chairing shed, where the chairbolts and chairs were placed in position using the pre-drilled holes before being placed on the chairing machine. This was essentially a large hydraulic press that pushed the chair into its seating using a force of about 9 tons. Whilst on the machine four hydraulic spanners would tighten the nuts, thus fixing the chair to the sleeper. The sleepers would then have one final check to ensure correctness of gauge before being loaded on to special sleeper wagons, each holding up to 155 chaired sleepers, which in turn would be stored in adjacent sidings until required.

The interior of the gauging shed at Hayes in 1912. Here chaired sleepers were tested for gauge prior to being loaded on to wagons. *Great Western Trust*

15. The Line Today

The area covered in this book has undergone considerable change over the last few years, not just in motive power but in the reconstruction and refurbishment of almost every station within the Thames and Chiltern line services.

Today Paddington is served by about 200 up and 200 down trains each 24hr and is used by about 60,000 passengers daily. Work is currently in progress on a £4.25 million refurbishment of the station roof. The work was started in 1987 and entails renewing the original wooden packing between the pillars and the roof structure, replacing the rooflights with polycarbon sheeting and finally redecorating the structure. It is envisaged that the present work should be completed during 1994. Recently a new £1.5 million fully computerised ticket office has been opened and a new passenger information centre has been installed on the 'Lawn'. This area should see further improvements in the near future with more retail outlets, better station seating and improved passenger facilities including the complete refurbishment of the ladies' toilet facilities on Platform No 1, (the gents' has already been completed). The cellars at Paddington are still being used for general storage; one store being of particular interest as it continues to be used by the GWR band, who currently give an evening concert on the 'Lawn' every Friday at 7.30pm.

In March 1992 a start was made on a £40 million scheme to alter the track layout and completely resignal the 4½-mile approach to Paddington. The scheme, which was undertaken jointly by InterCity and Network SouthEast, has replaced the existing two roads in, two roads out operations with six bi-directional tracks. All points and crossovers have been lengthened and many of the sharper curves have been flattened to allow higher approach speeds. All trackwork for a distance of about two miles out of Paddington has also been renewed. It is interesting to note that in order to straighten the

The 'Lawn' area and electronic arrival/departure display on 31 December 1992. As can be seen, this part of the roof has recently been refurbished. *Author*

Fulham and Kensington & Chelsea. It comprises a series of buildings which include a two-track bogie drop shed, a single-track wheel lathe shed, a six-track servicing shed and a four-road maintenance building. When fully operational it will provide servicing facilities for up to 18 Eurostar sets each evening. Incoming trains will enter the depot via a new incline connection from the West London line whilst outgoing trains will leave via what was the old Victoria Curve.

Apart from the new construction work, one of the biggest changes in recent years has been the introduction of new trains.

HST services in and out of Paddington have changed little since they were first introduced in 1976. Today, apart from the occasional extra, all of the main line services from Paddington to the West of England, South Wales, Bristol, Cheltenham and Worcester are operated by HSTs. However, since their introduction, and, apart from Slough where some main line services still stop, all other main line platforms on the intermediate stations between Paddington and Reading have either been removed or are now out of use.

It is on the suburban and intermediate services that the greatest change has taken place. During June 1992 new Network Turbo trains were introduced on to Thames line services and these, together with the introduction of new units on to Chiltern Line and Waterloo-Exeter services, have almost completely eliminated the use of Class 47s on passenger services into Paddington and Waterloo. The new units are serviced at new purpose-built depots at Reading, Aylesbury and Salisbury respectively. This has, of course, had a disastrous effect at Old Oak Common where the Class 47s used on these services were maintained; also from June 1993 maintenance of London-based HST sets has been switched to Bristol and Laira. This has, unfortunately, resulted in the closure of the heavy maintenance factory at Old Oak with the subsequent loss of 120 jobs.

The new Class 165 and 166 Turbo trains are certainly very efficient; they are quiet and smooth with good acceleration and apparently are particularly reliable, although it must be said the leg-room in the Class 165 units leaves a lot to be desired.

curve at Westbourne Park the main line station here was closed on 2 December 1991 and has since been removed. The new work has also seen the closure of Platform No 1A at Paddington. During the autumn of 1992 and the spring of 1993 up to six platforms at a time were temporarily closed at Paddington to allow the work to be undertaken. The signalling system is now controlled from the new integrated Electronic Control Centre at Slough. The opening of this new centre has allowed the closure of the panel box at Old Oak Common.

The new layout now allows a much greater track capacity for trains approaching the terminus. The actual platforming of trains at Paddington has seen little change. Generally InterCity services use Platforms Nos 1-7 and Network SouthEast Nos 10-14 with Nos 8 and 9 used by both. However, at busy times a certain amount of overlapping still occurs.

During the next few years a start should be made on the construction of the proposed £300 million 'Heathrow Express' link between Paddington and Heathrow airport. The new service will be operated using electric traction and

will have a journey time of about 16min. In anticipation of this the track levels have been lowered by about one foot, to allow room for the overhead equipment to pass under the bridges. This has been achieved by removing some 150,000 tons of ballast from under the track using special machines. The ballast was subsequently taken to Acton where it was stored in the old goods yard before being cleaned and reused. Although not yet finalised in seems that the new Heathrow services will operate from either Platforms Nos 1 and 2 or 6 and 7.

Another vast piece of construction work has recently been completed some two miles out of Paddington and alongside the Great Western main line at North Pole Junction. Here, in connection with the Channel Tunnel, a new £75 million servicing and maintenance depot for Eurostar trains has been constructed.

North Pole International Depot was opened on 11 November 1992 by the Chairman of British Rail, Sir Bob Reid. The new depot is actually some three kilometres in length and borders the boroughs of Ealing, Hammersmith &

Yeoman Class 59 No 59001 *Yeoman Endeavour* passes West Ealing with the 09.53 Crawley New Yard-Merehead empties on 30 April 1988. *Chris Wilson*

The Turbo units were first introduced on to Chiltern Line services to Banbury and Aylesbury to replace the ageing Class 115 Derby units during 1991. During the last few years this line has seen a considerable investment by Network SouthEast with £10 million being spent on the refurbishment of stations, £46 million on rolling stock and a further £12 million on signalling. Today the whole line is controlled via a new Integrated Electronic Control Centre at Marylebone, which was opened in April 1991. Services on the line now run to and from Marylebone and, during 1993, some services were extended to run through to Birmingham Snow Hill.

At the time of writing Class 165 Turbo units are being introduced on to Windsor, Marlow and Henley services, thus leaving only the Ealing-Greenford service still using Class 121 and Class 117 'Heritage' sets. For a number of years there have been no through services to Paddington from either Henley or Windsor, but the 1993 timetable saw the introduction of a new through 07.45 'Regatta Express' service between Henley and Paddington. Windsor also has its first through train for a number of years with the introduction of a through 'tourist' train which leaves Paddington at 10.20. Another train aimed specifically at the tourist trade is the 'Thames and Avon Express' to Stratford upon Avon. This service leaves Paddington at 09.20 and calls only at Oxford *en route*.

Delivery of the latest Class 166 Turbo Express units, of which 21 sets have been ordered, started in February 1993 and these have been gradually introduced on to the Paddington-Oxford/Worcester and Paddington-Newbury services.

Goods traffic in the area has altered considerably in the last 20 years or so and today comprises mostly stone, aggregates and oil traffic.

Almost all of the goods yards in the area covered by this book are now closed but, of those still open, Acton is now used by Railfreight Construction with regular daily services supplying the adjacent Foster Yeoman and Redland depots. There are also small stone and aggregate terminals at Westbourne Park (Tarmac and Marcon), Park Royal (Marcon), Hayes (Tarmac), West Dray-

ton (Amey Roadstone), Thorney Mill (Bardon Hill) and Brentford (Day & Son). These depots are individually supplied by services from a variety of locations including Merehead, Whatley, Croft and Bardon Hill Quarries. There is also a rubbish terminal at Brentford from where compacted waste is transferred on a daily basis to a tip at Appleford.

The two main oil terminals on the route are situated at Langley and Colnbrook and are currently supplied by services from Humber, Waterston and Immingham. Today the only coal traffic between Paddington and Twyford is to the coal concentration depot at West Drayton. This is currently served on Mondays, Wednesdays and Fridays by the 19.10 6B01S service from East Usk yard.

Another important plant is the Plasser Railway Machinery works at

West Ealing. Plasser, who supply most of the track maintenance equipment for BR, first set up their works at Ealing in 1969. The works are situated within the triangle of lines to Drayton Green Halt and Greenford. In 1977 the company started to construct machines on site and, in 1984, the facilities at West Ealing were extended with the construction of a large production shop. Today specialised track and electrification machines are manufactured at West Ealing for both this country and abroad.

On the new line between Old Oak Common and Ruislip just a few sidings remain. As already mentioned there is a Marcon stone terminal at Park Royal. One siding that continues to be busy serves the large Guinness complex at Park Royal. The company currently ships up to one third of its production at Park Royal by rail, supplying Scotland, the North of England and North Wales.

The 09.45 oil empties from the Total Oil depot at Langley to Waterston Sidings (Milford Haven) departs from Langley behind Class 60 No 60024 *Elizabeth Fry* on 22 June 1991. *Brian Morrison*

Class 56 No 56051 stands at the Bardon's discharge terminal at Thorney Mill on 19 February 1987. On this occasion the empties were returning to Frome, instead of the usual Leicestershire destination of Bardon Hill. This siding, together with the oil terminal at Colnbrook, are all that remains of the old Staines branch. *Paul Shannon*

Since the demise of Speedlink the company now runs its own daily service from Park Royal to Ordsall Lane Otis Euro Terminal (Crewe) from where the wagons are re-sorted. Guinness still maintain two ex-BR diesel shunters at Park Royal and these are used to shunt the company's extensive sidings.

The West London Waste Authority operate a refuse transfer station at Northolt. Compacted waste is currently transferred from here to a tip at Calvert, via the nightly 01.30 6A70S service.

Motive power on the goods services generally comprises Classes 56 and 59 on stone, 37, 47 and 60 on oil and 37 on coal. Other services are generally in the hands of Class 47s.

An exciting prospect for the future is the proposed Network SouthEast/London Underground 'Cross-Rail' link. When constructed the new line will link counties on either side of London to the City via a new twin tunnel underground system thus relieving congestion on current Network SouthEast and Central line services into East and West London. Trains from Reading and Aylesbury — the two western outer limits of the line — will use the existing surface tracks as far as Royal Oak where the new tunnel will begin. It is envisaged that new underground stations will be constructed at Paddington, Bond Street, Tottenham Court Road, Farringdon and Liverpool Street and, if everything goes to plan, the new railway could be in operation by 1999.

With the new trains, the imminent opening of the Channel Tunnel, the proposed 'Heathrow' and 'Cross-Rail' links and, of course, the privatisation proposals, the future of the Great Western line out of Paddington is about to enter a new phase. I wonder if he were still around today exactly what Brunel would have to say about it all?

Class 47 No 47838 departs from Old Oak Common carriage sidings via the flyover on 25 February 1990 with empty stock for a Paddington-Oxford service. Under the flyover is Class 50 No 50033 *Glorious* with the 9.30 Network Express service from Oxford. *Brian Morrison*

The old Staines branch now terminates at the Gulf Oil terminal at Colnbrook. Here, on 27 July 1992, Class 60 No 60062 *Samuel Johnson* is seen shortly after arriving with the 23.55 service from Waterston to Colnbrook. *Paul Shannon*

Class 56 No 56051 runs off the Brentford branch on 24 December 1990 with a special daytime working of the Brentford-Appleford rubbish train. This train normally runs overnight on weekdays and on Sunday mornings. *Paul Shannon*

Above:

Most main line services these days are operated using HSTs. Pictured at Subway Junction on 9 November 1991 are two HST sets. The nearer of the two, headed by No 43020 on the 09.35 Paddington-Plymouth, overtakes No 43161 *Reading Evening Post* on ECS for Old Oak Common. *Brian Morrison*

Left:

The Rail Express Parcels point at Paddington was opened on 1 October 1984. It is situated on what was the old cab road on the London Street side of the station. Notice the Red Star van decorated as a parcel. *Ian Allan Library*

The largest of the remaining rail-served plants is at the Guinness Park Royal Brewery. Today the company operates two '08' diesels to shunt the extensive sidings. These two shunters were purchased from BR in July 1985 and replaced the pair of 1949 Hibberds (see goods section). Here, on 29 January 1993, standing outside the small engine shed at Park Royal is *Unicorn* (ex-No 08060). The second '08', *Lion* (ex-No 08020) can just be seen inside the shed. *Author*

Class 47 No 47315 leaves the Guinness sidings at Park Royal on 19 April 1990 with the 15.12 Park Royal-Willesden Speedlink trip working. *Paul Shannon*

Class 37 No 37709 approaches Langley (Berks) with the 10.08 oil tanks from Micheldever to Ripple Lane on 22 June 1991. *Brian Morrison*

Above:
On 19 July 1990 Class 33 No 33023 approaches Acton with the 19.20 Topmix Cement service from Paddington New Yard to Plumstead. The Topmix terminal at Paddington is situated in what is left of the old goods yard at Westbourne Park. *Brian Morrison*

Left:
A pair of Thames Turbo units, Nos 165101 and 165126, stand under the heavily scaffolded roof at Paddington on 29 January 1993. *Author*

Below:
The scene at Old Oak Common carriage sidings on 8 February 1993. Many of the coaches and DMUs on view have been made redundant with the introduction of the new Turbo units. *Author*

Above:
Today almost all of the Thames line suburban services are in the hands of the Class 165/1 Turbo units. Passing through Ruscombe Cutting, near Twyford, on 19 September 1992 with the 12.00 service from Oxford to Paddington, are sets Nos 165113/107.
Brian Morrison

Right:
The interior of the new Eurostar maintenance building at North Pole shows some of the 27 lifting jacks.
Brian Morrison

Below right:
An exterior view of the six-road servicing shed at North Pole.
Brian Morrison

Facing page, top:
Today the remains of Paddington New Yard are used as a Marcon Stone terminal. Pictured here on 17 February 1993 is Class 60 No 60039 *Glastonbury Tor* shunting empty hoppers prior to departing with the 10.25 service to Angerstein Wharf. *Paul Shannon*

Facing page, bottom:
As part of the Thames line modernisation work the old staggered up relief platform at West Ealing has been removed. This view, taken on 11 March 1992 from the new up relief platform, shows Class 119 set No L580 (Nos 51094, 59425, 51066) approaching with the 12.50 Paddington-Slough service. *Brian Morrison*

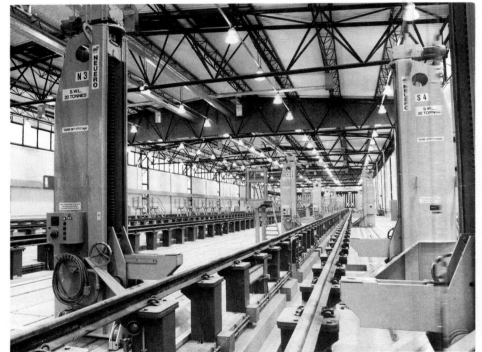

Appendices

1. Opening/closing dates of stations

Main Line

	Opened	Closed
Paddington (Old)	4/6/1838	29/5/1854
Paddington (New)	29/5/1854	
Bishop's Road	10/1/1863*	
Royal Oak	30/10/1871	
Westbourne Park	1/2/1866	2/12/1991
Acton	1/2/1868	
Ealing Broadway	1/12/1838	
Castle Hill, Ealing	1/3/1871	
(West Ealing from 1/7/1899)		
Hanwell & Elthorne	1/12/1838	
Southall	1/5/1839	
Hayes and Harlington	1/5/1864	
West Drayton	4/6/1838	
Iver	1/12/1924	
Langley	1/12/1845	
Slough	4/6/1841	
Burnham Beeches	1/7/1899	
Taplow	1/9/1872	
Maidenhead (1st)	4/6/1838	1/9/1872
Maidenhead	1/11/1871	
Twyford	1/7/1839	

* Bishop's Road Station to Paddington Suburban 10/9/33.

Branches

Brentford Branch
	Opened	Closed
Trumpers Crossing Halt	1/7/1904	30/1/1926
Brentford Town	1/5/1860	2/5/1942

Staines Branch
	Opened	Closed
Colnbrook Estate Halt	1/5/1961	29/3/1965
Colnbrook	9/8/1884	29/3/1965
Poyle Estate Halt	1/4/1954	29/3/1965
Poyle Halt	1/6/1927	29/3/1965
Runemede Halt	1/4/1887	14/5/1962
(Yeoveney Halt from 4/11/1935)		
Staines West	2/11/1885	29/3/1965

Windsor Branch
	Opened	Closed
Chalvey Halt	6/5/1929	6/7/1930
Windsor		

Uxbridge Branch
	Opened	Closed
Cowley	2/10/1904	10/9/1962
Uxbridge Vine Street	8/9/1856	10/9/1962
Uxbridge High Street	1/5/1907	1/9/1939

Henley Branch
	Opened	Closed
Wargrave	1/1/1900	
Shiplake	1/6/1857	
Henley on Thames	1/6/1857	

Wycombe/Marlow Branch
	Opened	Closed
Furze Platt Halt	5/7/1937	
Cookham	1/8/1854	
Marlow Road	1/8/1854	
(Bourne End from 1/1/74)		
Wooburn Green	1/8/1854	5/1970
Loudwater	1/8/1854	5/1970
Great Marlow	27/6/1873	
(Bourne End from 1/1/18)		

Greenford Loop
	Opened	Closed
South Greenford	20/9/1926	
Castle Bar Park Halt	1/5/1904	
Drayton Green	1/3/1905	

Great Western/ Great Central Joint
	Opened	Closed
Old Oak Lane Halt	1/10/1906	29/6/1947
North Acton	5/11/1923	29/6/1947
North Acton Halt	1/5/1904	31/1/1913
Park Royal	15/6/1903	26/6/1937
Park Royal West Halt	20/6/1932	29/6/1947
Twyford Abbey	1/5/1904	30/4/1911
Brentham Halt	1/5/1911	29/5/1947
Perivale Halt	1/5/1904	29/5/1947
Greenford	1/10/1904	17/5/1963*
Northolt Halt	1/5/1907	21/11/1948
Northolt Junc	1/7/1908	
(South Ruislip from 12/9/1932)		
Ruislip Gardens	9/7/1934	21/6/1958
Ruislip & Ickenham	2/4/1906	
(West Ruislip from 30/6/1947)		
South Harefield Halt	24/9/1928	1/10/1931
Denham	2/4/1906	
Denham Golf Club Halt	7/12/1912	
Gerrards Cross	2/4/1906	
Beaconsfield Golf Links Halt	23/12/1914	
(Seer Green and Jordans from 1/1/1919)		
Beaconsfield	2/4/1906	

* Great Western station. Bay platform at Central line station now used.

West London Railway
	Opened	Closed
St Quintin Park & Wormwood Scrubs	1/8/1871	21/10/1940
Uxbridge Road	1/11/1869	21/10/1940
Kensington Addison Rd (Olympia)	2/3/1863	
West Brompton	1/9/1866	21/10/1940
Chelsea & Fulham	2/3/1863	21/10/1940
Battersea	2/3/1863	21/10/1940

2. Locomotive Allocations

The following locomotive allocations give a fair indication of the type of motive power used over the years within the area covered by this book. Of the locomotive depots in this section, Paddington provided locomotives for both main line and suburban services, Slough was basically a suburban shed whilst Southall although providing motive power for some suburban and branch services, was essentially a freight shed.

Paddington (Westbourne Park)

1 January 1901

Armstrong 4-4-0 class: 8 *Gooch*, 14 *Brunel*, 16 *Charles Saunders*

'Queen' class 2-2-2: 55 *Queen*, 1118 *Prince Christian*, 1119 *Princess of Wales*, 1124, 1125, 1128 *Duke of York*, 1131, 1132 *Prince of Wales*

'131' class 0-6-0: 145

388 class standard goods 0-6-0: 51, 506

'455' class 'Metro' 2-4-0T: 613, 1401, 1403, 1405, 1407, 1411, 1412, 1415, 1418, 1419, 3561, 3562, 3563, 3565, 3567, 3568, 3569, 3585, 3586, 3592, 3595, 3597, 3598, 3599

'850'/'1901' class 0-6-0ST: 854, 866, 868, 870, 1221, 1905, 1906, 1910, 1911, 1915, 1934, 1935, 1967, 1970, 1976, 1985, 1996

'1016' class 0-6-0ST: 1068

'1076' class 0-6-0ST: 734, 735

'1661' class 0-6-0ST: 1674

'2021' class 0-6-0ST: 2074, 2075

'2301' class 'Dean Goods': 2313, 2358, 2383, 2384, 2389, 2396, 2398, 2433, 2450, 2455, 2459, 2473, 2480, 2487

'3031' 'Achilles' class 4-2-2: 3004 *Black Prince*, 3006 *Courier*, 3010 *Fire King*, 3012 *Great Western*, 3016 *Lightning*, 3021 *Wigmore Castle*, 3026 *Tornado*, 3031 *Achilles*, 3032 *Agamemnon*, 3034 *Behemoth*, 3035 *Beaufort*, 3038 *Livonia*, 3040 *Empress of India*, 3044 *Hurricane*, 3046 *Lord of the Isles*, 3050 *Royal Sovereign*, 3051 *Stormy Petrel*, 3058 *Grierson*, 3061 *Alexandra*, 3068 *Duke of Cambridge*, 3073 *Princess Royal*, 3075 *Princess Louise*, 3076 *Princess Beatrice*, 3077 *Shooting Star*

'3201' class 2-4-0: 3203

'3232' class 2-4-0: 3233, 3236

'3252' 'Duke' class 4-4-0: 3254 *Boscawen*, 3259 *Lizard*, 3262 *Powderham*, 3265 *St Germans*, 3270 *Trevithick*, 3273 *Armorel*, 3276 *Dartmoor*, 3277 *Earl of Devon*, 3279 *Exmoor*, 3280 *Falmouth*, 3281 *Fowey*, 3283 *Mounts Bay*, 3284 *Newquay*, 3286 *St Just*, 3289 *Trefusis*, 3291 *Tregenna*

'3292' 'Badminton' class 4-4-0: 3292 *Badminton*, 3293 *Barrington*, 3294 *Blenheim*, 3295 *Bessborough*, 3297 *Earl Cawdor*, 3298 *Grosvenor*, 3299 *Hubbard*, 3304 *Oxford*, 3323 *Mendip*, 3324 *Quantock*

'Bulldog' class 4-4-0: 3341 *Mars*, 3367 *St Aubyn*

'Atbara' class 4-4-0: 3374 *Baden Powell*, 3383 *Kekewich*, 3387 *Roberts*, 3392 *White*

Total 134

Paddington (Old Oak Common)

1 January 1920

'455' class 'Metro' 2-4-0T: 616, 3567, 3568, 3570, 3586, 3591, 3592

'633' class 0-6-0T: 634, 641, 642, 643

'655' class 0-6-0T: 1789

'1076' class 0-6-0T: 738, 748, 1081, 1230, 1295, 1567, 1597, 1634, 1639, 1651

'850'/'1901' class 0-6-0T: 868, 990, 992, 1217, 1219, 1226, 1901, 1906, 1908, 1911, 1946, 1961, 1966, 1969, 1970, 1972, 1974, 1975, 1987, 1994, 2000

'1701'/'1854' class 0-6-0T: 1722, 1729, 1792, 1870, 1889

'1813' class 0-6-0T: 1849, 1850

'2021' class 0-6-0T: 2026, 2037, 2038, 2046, 2075, 2097

'2221' class 4-4-2T: 2222, 2224, 2226, 2227, 2228, 2229, 2230, 2231, 2234, 2243, 2244, 2247, 2250

'2301' class 'Dean Goods' 0-6-0: 2384, 2409, 2417, 2455, 2484, 2515, 2556

'26xx' class 'Aberdare' 2-6-0: 2604, 2659

'2721' class 0-6-0T: 2767, 2779, 2781, 2792

'28xx' class 2-8-0: 2874, 2881

'29xx' 'Saint' class 4-6-0: 2901 *Lady Superior*, 2904 *Lady Godiva*, 2906 *Lady of Lynn*, 2920 *Saint David*, 2944 *Highnam Court*, 2979 *Quentin Durward*, 2989 *Talisman*

'30xx' class ex-ROD 2-8-0: 3005, 3006, 3007, 3008, 3010, 3014

'33xx' 'Bulldog' class 4-4-0: 3394 *Albany*, 3429, 3434 *Joseph Shaw*

'36xx' class 2-4-2T: 3600, 3614, 3615, 3617, 3619

'37xx' 'City' class 4-4-0: 3709 *Quebec*

'38xx' 'County' class 4-4-0: 3800 *County of Middlesex*, 3809 *County Wexford*, 3820 *County of Worcester*, 3828 *County of Hereford*, 3835 *County of Devon*, 3838 *County of Glamorgan*

'40xx' 'Star' class 4-6-0: 4000 *North Star*, 4001 *Dog Star*, 4002 *Evening Star*, 4003 *Lode Star*, 4007 *Rising Star*, 4010 *Western Star*, 4011 *Knight of the Garter*, 4012 *Knight of the Thistle*, 4013 *Knight of St Patrick*, 4014 *Knight of the Bath*, 4021 *King Edward*, 4023 *King George*, 4027 *King Henry*, 4029 *King Stephen*, 4031 *Queen Mary*, 4032 *Queen Alexandra*, 4033 *Queen Victoria*, 4034 *Queen Adelaide*, 4036 *Queen Elizabeth*, 4037 *Queen Philippa*, 4042 *Prince Henry*, 4047 *Princess Louise*, 4048 *Princess Victoria*, 4055 *Princess Sophia*, 4056 *Princess Margaret*, 4059 *Princess Patricia*

'4120' 'Atbara' class 4-4-0: 4138 *White*

'43xx' class 2-6-0: 4359, 4363, 4368, 4371, 4372, 4387, 5305, 5306, 5348, 5350, 5351, 5354, 5359, 5362

Ex-LBSCR 'C2X' class 0-6-0T: 524, 527,

Total: 156

Paddington (Old Oak Common)

1 January 1930

'455' class 'Metro' 2-4-0T: 3567, 3568, 3570, 3585, 3586, 3591, 3592

'633' class 0-6-0T: 633, 634, 641, 642, 643

'850' class 0-6-0T: 852, 1217, 1903, 1946, 1969, 1996

'1016' class 0-6-0T: 1060, 1062

'1076' class 0-6-0T: 1081, 1152, 1175, 1257, 1651

'1813' class 0-6-0T: 1817, 1836

'1854' class 0-6-0T: 1857, 1872

'2021' class 0-6-0T: 2038, 2046, 2081, 2083

'2221' class 4-4-2T: 2224, 2230, 2232, 2234, 2235, 2236, 2244, 2247, 2248

'2301' class 'Dean Goods' 0-6-0: 2484, 2515

'2361' class 0-6-0: 2362, 2370

'2600' class 'Aberdare' 2-6-0: 2611, 2626, 2653

'2721' class 0-6-0T: 2752

'28xx' class 2-8-0: 2805, 2816, 2820, 2846, 2847, 2864, 2867, 2879

'29xx' class 'Saint' 4-6-0: 2952 *Twineham Court*, 2980 *Coeur de Lion*

'30xx' class ex-ROD 2-8-0: 3020, 3023, 3047

'3252' class 4-4-0: 3274 *Newquay*

'33xx' class 'Bulldog' 4-4-0: 3341 *Blasius*, 3374 *Walter Long*, 3407 *Madras*, 3429

'36xx' class 2-4-2T: 3612, 3619, 3626

'40xx' class 'Star' 4-6-0: 4005 *Polar Star*, 4007 *Rising Star*, 4017 *Knight of Liege*, 4020 *Knight Commander*, 4038 *Queen Berengaria*, 4041 *Prince of Wales*, 4043 *Prince Henry*, 4046 *Princess Mary*, 4053 *Princess Alexandra*, 4054 *Princess Charlotte*, 4055 *Princess Sophia*, 4059 *Princess Patricia*, 4064 *Reading Abbey*, 4072 *Tresco Abbey*

'4073' class 'Castle' 4-6-0: 111 *The Great Bear*, 4037 *Queen Philippa*, 4073 *Caerphilly Castle*, 4074 *Caldicot Castle*, 4076 *Carmarthen Castle*, 4078 *Pembroke Castle*, 4079 *Pendennis Castle*, 4081 *Warwick Castle*, 4083 *Abbotsbury Castle*, 4089 *Donnington Castle*, 4090

Dorchester Castle, 4091 *Dudley Castle*, 4092 *Dunraven Castle*, 4093 *Dunster Castle*, 4099 *Kilgerran Castle*, 5000 *Launceston Castle*, 5001 *Llandovery Castle*, 5003 *Lulworth Castle*, 5005 *Manorbier Castle*, 5006 *Tregenna Castle*, 5009 *Shrewsbury Castle*, 5010 *Restormel Castle*

'43xx' class 2-6-0: 4331, 4365, 4382, 4384, 4396, 5321, 5380, 6310, 6318, 6330, 6332, 6354, 6362, 6367, 6373, 6378, 6388, 6392, 7312, 7319, 7321, 8304, 8333, 8360, 8365, 8366, 8387

'45xx' class 2-6-2T: 4519, 4521, 4522, 4557, 4563, 4567, 4568, 4571

'47xx' class 2-8-0: 4701, 4702, 4703, 4705, 4708

'49xx' 'Hall' class 4-6-0: 4900 *Saint Martin*, 4921 *Eaton Hall*, 4922 *Enville Hall*, 4924 *Eydon Hall*, 4925 *Eynsham Hall*, 4926 *Fairleigh Hall*, 4927 *Farnborough Hall*, 4943 *Marrington Hall*, 4944 *Middleton Hall*, 4951 *Pendeford Hall*, 4968 *Shotton Hall*, 4969 *Shugborough Hall*, 4970 *Sketty Hall*

'51xx' class 2-6-2T: 5119, 5123, 5141, 5149

'57xx' class 0-6-0PT: 5715, 5717, 5737, 5745, 5750, 5751, 5752, 5753, 5754, 5757, 5758, 5759, 5760, 5761, 5762, 5763, 5764, 5765, 5766, 5767, 5772, 5773, 5779, 7731

'60xx' 'King' class 4-6-0: 6000 *King George V*, 6001 *King Edward VII*, 6003 *King George IV*, 6005 *King George II*, 6007 *King William III*, 6009 *King Charles II*, 6011 *King James I*, 6013 *King Henry VIII*, 6015 *King Richard III*

Department Sentinel 0-4-0: 13

Total: 198

Paddington (Old Oak Common)

1 January 1940

'850' class 0-6-0PT: 1912, 1969
'2301' class 'Dean Goods' 0-6-0: 2395
'2361' class 0-6-0: 2381
'28xx' class 2-8-0: 2826, 2840, 2843, 2848, 2850, 2855, 2863, 2868, 2875, 2881
'4073' 'Castle' class 4-6-0: 100A1 *Lloyds*, 111 *The Great Bear*, 4037 *The South Wales Borderers*, 4073 *Caerphilly Castle*, 4075 *Cardiff Castle*, 4082 *Windsor Castle*, 4091 *Dudley Castle*, 5000 *Launceston Castle*, 5004 *Llanstephan Castle*, 5005 *Manorbier Castle*, 5008 *Raglan Castle*, 5018 *St Mawes Castle*, 5019 *Treago Castle*, 5022 *Wigmore Castle*, 5023 *Brecon Castle*, 5027 *Farleigh Castle*, 5029 *Nunney Castle*, 5036 *Lyonshall Castle*, 5037 *Monmouth Castle*, 5038 *Morlais Castle*, 5039 *Rhuddlan Castle*, 5040 *Stokesay Castle*, 5043 *Earl of Mount Edgcumbe*, 5044 *Earl of Dunraven*, 5045 *Earl of Dudley*, 5055 *Earl of Eldon*, 5056 *Earl of Powis*, 5066 *Wardour Castle*, 5067 *St Fagans Castle*, 5069 *Isambard Kingdom Brunel*, 5079 *Lydford Castle*, 5080 *Ogmore Castle*, 5085 *Evesham Abbey*, 5093 *Upton Castle*

'43xx' class 2-6-0: 5321, 6388, 9302, 9306, 9307, 9308, 9311
'47xx' class 2-8-0: 4700, 4701, 4702, 4705, 4707
'49xx' 'Hall' class 4-6-0: 4900 *St Martin*, 4907 *Broughton Hall*, 4935 *Ketley Hall*, 4936 *Kinlet Hall*, 4938 *Liddington Hall*, 4943 *Marrington Hall*, 4961 *Pyrland Hall*, 4973 *Sweeney Hall*, 4978 *Westwood Hall*, 4981 *Abberley Hall*, 4985 *Allesley Hall*, 4998 *Eydon Hall*, 5903 *Keele Hall*, 5922 *Caxton Hall*, 5931 *Hatherley Hall*, 5934 *Kneller Hall*, 5936 *Oakley Hall*, 5937 *Stanford Hall*, 5938 *Stanley Hall*, 5939 *Tangley Hall*, 5940 *Whitbourne Hall*, 5941 *Campion Hall*, 5950 *Wardley Hall*, 5954 *Faendre Hall*, 5955 *Garth Hall*, 5962 *Wantage Hall*, 5978 *Bodinnick Hall*, 5985 *Mostyn Hall*, 5987 *Brocket Hall*

'57xx' class 0-6-0PT: 3600, 3618, 3619, 3635, 3642, 3644, 3646, 3648, 3710, 3734, 3738, 3754, 3766, 5717, 5750, 5751, 5752, 5753, 5764, 5765, 5779, 5799, 7713, 7734, 7754, 7760, 8707, 8750, 8751, 8753, 8754, 8756, 8757, 8759, 8760, 8761, 8762, 8763, 8765, 8767, 8768, 8769, 8770, 8771, 8772, 8773, 9700, 9701, 9702, 9703, 9704, 9705, 9706, 9707, 9708, 9709, 9710, 9725, 9726, 9749, 9751, 9754, 9758, 9784

'60xx' 'King' class 4-6-0: 6001 *King Edward VII* 6003 *King George IV*, 6007 *King William III*, 6009 *King Charles II*,

6013 *King Henry VIII*, 6014 *King Henry VII*, 6015 *King Richard III*, 6021 *King Richard II*, 6025 *King Henry III*, 6027 *King Richard I*, 6028 *King George VI*
'61xx' class 2-6-2T: 6107, 6111, 6120, 6121, 6132, 6134, 6137, 6141, 6142, 6144, 6155, 6166
'68xx' 'Grange' class 4-6-0: 6802 *Bampton Grange*, 6809 *Burghclere Grange*, 6826 *Nannerth Grange*, 6854 *Dymock Grange*, 6865 *Hopton Grange*
Departmental Sentinel 0-4-0: 13

Total: 182

Paddington (Old Oak Common)

1 January 1950

'10xx' 'County' class 4-6-0: 1000 *County of Middlesex*, 1003 *County of Wilts*, 1008 *County of Cardigan*, 1011 *County of Caernarvon*, 1012 *County of Denbigh*, 1015 *County of Gloucester*, 1021 *County of Montgomery*, 1026 *County of Salop*
'15xx' class 0-6-0PT: 1500, 1501, 1502, 1503, 1504, 1505
'2251' class 0-6-0: 2276, 2282
'28xx/2885' class 2-8-0: 2826, 2868, 2895, 3813, 3852, 3853
'30xx' class ex-ROD 2-8-0: 3017
'4073' 'Castle' class 4-6-0: 4075 *Cardiff Castle*, 5004 *Llanstephan Castle*, 5014 *Goodrich Castle*, 5027 *Farleigh Castle*, 5029 *Nunney Castle*, 5035 *Coity Castle*, 5038 *Morlais Castle*, 5039 *Rhuddlan Castle*, 5040 *Stokesay Castle*, 5043 *Earl of Mount Edgcumbe*, 5044 *Earl of Dunraven*, 5045 *Earl of Dudley*, 5055 *Earl of Eldon*, 5056 *Earl of Powis*, 5065 *Newport Castle*, 5066 *Wardour Castle*, 5069 *Isambard Kingdom Brunel*, 5081 *Lockheed Hudson*, 5085 *Evesham Abbey*, 5087 *Tintern Abbey*, 7001 *Sir James Milne*, 7004 *Eastnor Castle*, 7013 *Bristol Castle*, 7024 *Powis Castle*, 7025 *Sudeley Castle*, 7030 *Cranbrook Castle*, 7032 *Denbigh Castle*, 7033 *Hartlebury Castle*

'43xx' class 2-6-0: 9302, 9304, 9305, 9306, 9308, 9309, 9315
'47xx' class 2-8-0: 4700, 4701, 4702, 4705, 4707
'49xx' 'Hall' class 4-6-0: 4900 *St Martin*, 4923 *Evenley Hall*, 4958 *Priory Hall*, 4961 *Pyrland Hall*, 5918 *Walton Hall*, 5931 *Hatherley Hall*, 5932 *Haydon Hall*, 5936 *Oakley Hall*, 5937 *Stanford Hall*, 5938 *Stanley Hall*, 5939 *Tangley Hall*, 5940 *Whitbourne Hall*, 5941 *Campion Hall*, 5947 *Saint Benet's Hall*, 5952 *Cogan Hall*, 5962 *Wantage Hall*, 5986 *Arbury Hall*, 5987 *Brocket Hall*, 5996 *Mytton Hall*, 6900 *Abney Hall*, 6910 *Gossington Hall*, 6926 *Holkham Hall*, 6932 *Burwarton Hall*, 6944 *Fledborough Hall*, 6953 *Leighton Hall*

'57xx' class 0-6-0PT: 3648, 3685, 3688, 3710, 3754, 4615, 4644, 4666, 4698, 4699, 5764, 7734, 7791, 8750, 8751, 8753, 8754, 8756, 8757, 8759, 8760, 8761, 8762, 8763, 8764, 8765, 8767, 8768, 8769, 8770, 8771, 8772, 8773, 9658, 9659, 9661, 9700, 9701, 9702, 9703, 9704, 9705, 9706, 9707, 9708, 9709, 9710, 9725, 9751, 9754, 9758, 9784

'60xx' 'King' class 4-6-0: 6001 *King Edward VII*, 6002 *King William IV*, 6003 *King George IV*, 6007 *King William III*, 6009 *King Charles II*, 6013 *King Henry VIII*, 6014 *King Henry VII*, 6015 *King Richard III*, 6017 *King Edward IV*, 6018 *King Henry VI*, 6019 *King Henry V*, 6021 *King Richard I*, 6028 *King George VI*
'61xx' class 2-6-2T: 6117, 6120, 6121, 6135, 6137, 6141, 6142, 6144, 6149, 6155, 6158, 6159, 6168
'6959' 'Modified Hall' class 4-6-0: 6959 *Peatling Hall*, 6960 *Raveningham Hall*, 6962 Soughton *Hall*, 6973 *Bricklehampton* Hall, 6974 *Bryngwyn Hall*, 6983 *Otterington Hall*, 6985 *Parwick Hall*, 6990 *Witherslack Hall*, 7902 *Eaton Mascot Hall*, 7903 *Foremarke Hall*, 7904 *Fountains Hall*, 7911 *Lady Margaret Hall*
'94xx' class 0-6-0PT: 9401, 9402, 9403, 9404, 9405, 9406, 9418, 9419, 9422
Ex-WD 2-8-0: 90101, 90105
0-6-0 Diesel-Electric: 15101, 15102, 15103, 15104, 15105, 15106
Gas Turbine: 18000

Total: 188

Paddington (Old Oak Common)
1 January 1960

'15xx' class 0-6-0PT: 1500, 1503, 1504, 1505

'2251' class 0-6-0: 2222, 2276, 2282

'4073' 'Castle' class 4-6-0: 4075 *Cardiff Castle*, 4082 *Windsor Castle*, 4096 *Highclere Castle*, 5008 *Raglan Castle*, 5014 *Goodrich Castle*, 5027 *Farleigh Castle*, 5034 *Corfe Castle*, 5040 *Stokesay Castle*, 5043 *Earl of Mount Edgcumbe*, 5044 *Earl of Dunraven*, 5052 *Earl of Radnor*, 5056 *Earl of Powis*, 5060 *Earl of Berkeley*, 5065 *Newport Castle*, 5066 *Sir Felix Pole*, 5074 *Wellington*, 5082 *Swordfish*, 5084 *Reading Abbey*, 5087 *Tintern Abbey*, 7001 *Sir James Milne*, 7004 *Eastnor Castle*, 7010 *Avondale Castle*, 7013 *Bristol Castle*, 7017 *G. J. Churchward*, 7020 *Gloucester Castle*, 7024 *Powis Castle*, 7025 *Sudeley Castle*, 7030 *Cranbrook Castle*, 7032 *Denbigh Castle*, 7033 *Hartlebury Castle*, 7036 *Taunton Castle*

'47xx' class 2-8-0: 4700, 4701, 4702, 4704, 4708

'49xx' 'Hall' class 4-6-0: 4919 *Donnington Hall*, 5907 *Marble Hall*, 5923 *Colston Hall*, 5929 *Hanham Hall*, 5931 *Hatherley Hall*, 5932 *Haydon Hall*, 5939 *Tangley Hall*, 5954 *Faendre Hall*, 5958 *Knolton Hall*, 5976 *Ashwicke Hall*, 5987 *Brocket Hall*, 6920 *Barningham Hall*, 6942 *Eshton Hall*

'57xx' class 0-6-0PT: 3648, 3688, 3754, 4615, 4644, 5717, 5764, 7722, 8751, 8753, 8754, 8756, 8757, 8759, 8760, 8762, 8763, 8764, 8765, 8767, 8768, 8770, 8771, 8772, 8773, 9658, 9659, 9661, 9701, 9702, 9703, 9704, 9705, 9706, 9707, 9709, 9710, 9725, 9751, 9754, 9758, 9784

'60xx' 'King' class 4-6-0: 6000 *King George V*, 6003 *King George IV*, 6004 *King George III*, 6009 *King Charles II*, 6010 *King Charles I*, 6012 *King Edward VI*, 6013 *King Henry VIII*, 6015 *King Richard III*, 6018 *King Henry VI*, 6019 *King Henry V*, 6021 *King Richard II*, 6023 *King Edward II*, 6024 *King Edward I*, 6025 *King Henry III*, 6026 *King John*, 6028 *King George VI*, 6029 *King Edward VIII*

'61xx' class 2-6-2T: 6108, 6113, 6120, 6121, 6132, 6135, 6141, 6142, 6144, 6145, 6158, 6163, 6168

'6959' 'Modified Hall' class 4-6-0: 6959 *Peatling Hall*, 6961 *Stedham Hall*, 6962 *Soughton Hall*, 6966 *Witchingham Hall*, 6973 *Bricklehampton Hall*, 6974 *Bryngwyn Hall*, 6978 *Haroldstone Hall*, 6990 *Witherslack Hall*, 7902 *Eaton Mascot Hall*, 7903 *Foremarke Hall*, 7904 *Fountains Hall*, 7927 *Willington Hall*

'94xx' class 0-6-0PT: 8459, 9405, 9410, 9411, 9412, 9414, 9416, 9418, 9419, 9420, 9423, 9469, 9479

Ex-LMS '8F' 2-8-0: 48410, 48412, 48431

BR Standard Class 9F 2-10-0 92211, 92229, 92230, 92238, 92239, 92240, 92241, 92244, 92245, 92246, 92247

Class 08 Diesel D3030, D3031, D3032, D3033, D3406, D3512, D3597, D3598, D3599, D3600, D3601, D3602, D3604, D3758, D3759, D3760, D3947, D3948, D3949, D3950, D3951, D3952, D3953, D3954, D3955

Final steam allocation June 1964.

'94xx' class 0-6-0PT: 8420, 8433, 9411, 9415

Total: 192

Old Oak Diesel Depot
1970

Class 08 3598, 3599, 3600, 3601, 3602, 3605, 3754, 3756, 3761, 3762, 3947, 3954, 3955, 3961, 3962, 3963, 3965, 3966, 3972, 3999, 4000, 4003, 4006, 4026

Class 22 6326, 6327, 6328, 6332, 6336, 6340, 6343

Class 31 5528, 5530, 5535, 5536, 5539

Class 35 7026, 7027, 7028, 7029, 7030, 7034, 7035, 7036, 7045, 7046, 7050, 7058, 7061, 7062, 7065, 7066, 7071, 7072

Class 42/43 'Warship' 833 *Panther*, 835 *Pegasus*, 837 *Ramillies*, 841 *Roebuck*, 843 *Sharpshooter*, 846 *Steadfast*, 849 *Superb*, 850 *Swift*, 853 *Thruster*, 855 *Triumph*

Class 47 1583, 1587, 1594, 1596, 1636, 1637, 1638, 1639, 1640, 1641, 1648, 1649, 1652, 1653, 1670, 1674 *Samson*, 1675 *Amazon*, 1678, 1679, 1680, 1681

Total: 85

Old Oak Commom
1980

Class 08 08480, 08630, 08651, 08785, 08793, 08794, 08797, 08798, 08825, 08936, 08944, 08947, 08948

Class 31 31117, 31121, 31124, 31132, 31135, 31158, 31163, 31209, 31213, 31230, 31241, 31259, 31260, 31273, 31304, 31412, 31413, 31414, 31415, 31416, 31423, 31424

Class 47 47054, 47055, 47056, 47059, 47060, 47061, 47063, 47066, 47500 *Great Western*, 47508 *Great Britain*, 47509 *Albion*, 47510, 47511 *Thames*, 47513 *Severn*

Class 50 50028 *Tiger*, 50029 *Renown*, 50030 *Repulse*, 50031 *Hood*, 50032 *Courageous*, 50033 *Glorious*, 50034 *Furious*, 50035 *Ark Royal*, 50036 *Victorious*, 50048 *Dauntless*

Total: 59

Old Oak Common
February 1993

Class 08 08454, 08460, 08480, 08651, 08653, 08825, 08837, 08887, 08904, 08944, 08947, 08948

Class 43 HST powercars 43140, 43141, 43142, 43144, 43145, 43146, 43147 *The Red Cross*, 43148

Class 47 47004, 47019, 47105, 47108, 47121, 47315, 47334, 47364, 47366, 47431, 47449, 47484 *Isambard Kingdom Brunel*, 47526, 47579 *James Nightall GC*, 47583 *County of Hertfordshire*, 47701 *Old Oak Common Traction & Rolling Stock Depot*, 47702 *Saint Cuthbert*, 47705, 47706, 47707 *Holyrood*, 47708 *Templecombe*, 47709, 47711, 47712 *Lady Diana Spencer*, 47714, 47715 *Haymarket*, 47716 *Duke of Edinburgh's Award*, 47717

Total: 48

Slough
1 January 1901

'455' class 'Metro' 2-4-0T: 4, 5, 6, 466, 467, 618, 619, 967, 968, 972, 975, 976, 977, 978, 981, 984, 985, 1445, 1447

Armstrong '388' class 0-6-0: 1206

'2301' class 'Dean goods' 0-6-0: 2314, 2503

'517' class 0-4-2T: 1160

Total: 23

Slough
1 January 1920

Armstrong '388' class 0-6-0: 707

'455' class 'Metro' 2-4-0T: 1408, 3564, 3566, 3569, 3581, 3584, 3587, 3596

'806' class 2-4-0: 812

'2221' class 4-4-2T 'County': 2221, 2223, 2225, 2232, 2237, 2240, 2242, 2245, 2248, 2249

'3232' class 2-4-0: 3247

'36xx' class 2-4-2T: 3601, 3606, 3626

'2301' 'Dean Goods' 0-6-0: 2343

'2021' class 0-6-0ST/PT: 2121, 2137

'1076' class 0-6-0ST/PT: 1179

Total: 28

Slough
1 January 1930

'455' class 'Metro' 2-4-0T: 972, 1403, 1407, 1497, 3500, 3563, 3564, 3569, 3588, 3589, 3595

'2021' class 0-6-0T: 2026, 2069, 2087, 2112

'2221' class 4-4-2T: 2222, 2223, 2225, 2226, 2227, 2228, 2231, 2238, 2239, 2240, 2241, 2242, 2243, 2245

'2301' class 'Dean Goods' 0-6-0: 2312

'2721' class 0-6-0T: 2787

'33xx' class 'Bulldog' 4-4-0: 3410 *Columbia*

'36xx' class 2-4-2T: 3601, 3617

'39xx' class 2-6-2T: 3907

'56xx' class 0-6-2T: 6670, 6671

Steam Railmotor: 55, 64

Total: 39

Slough

1 January 1940
'2021' class 0-6-0PT: 2078
'2721' class 0-6-0PT: 2747, 2757
'48xx' class 0-4-2T: 4807, 4831
'57xx' class 0-6-0PT: 3769, 5715, 5783, 9763, 9789
'6100' class 2-6-2T: 6101, 6102, 6104, 6105, 6108, 6113, 6114, 6116, 6119, 6123, 6124, 6126, 6127, 6133, 6143, 6145, 6149, 6150, 6151, 6152, 6157, 6160, 6161, 6164, 6167

Total: 36

Slough

1 January 1950
'48xx' class 0-4-2T: 1437, 1442
'2021' class 0-6-0PT: 2112
'57xx' class 0-6-0PT: 3738, 4606, 4650, 4691, 5715, 5717, 5737, 5783, 9640, 9653, 9781, 9789
'54xx' class 0-6-0PT: 5409
'61xx' class 2-6-2T: 6104, 6106, 6107, 6108, 6113, 6114, 6115, 6116, 6119, 6123, 6124, 6127, 6131, 6133, 6136, 6140, 6143, 6146, 6150, 6151, 6152, 6154, 6157, 6160, 6161, 6164
'74xx' class 0-6-0PT: 7441, 7442
'94xx' class 0-6-0PT: 9414, 9415, 9421, 9424

Total: 48

Slough

1 January 1960
'48xx' class 0-4-2T: 1447, 1448
'57xx' class 0-6-0PT: 3608, 4606, 4638, 4650, 5755, 5766, 9722, 9781
'61xx' class 2-6-2T: 6108, 6109, 6117, 6123, 6124, 6126, 6127, 6133, 6136, 6143, 6146, 6150, 6151, 6152, 6154, 6164, 6167
'56xx' class 0-6-2T: 6655
'94xx' class 0-6-0PT: 9406, 9415, 9421, 9424

Total: 32

Slough

Final steam allocation June 1964
'16xx' class 0-6-0PT: 1622, 1654
'61xx' class 2-6-2T: 6117, 6128, 6143, 6160, 6167

Total: 7

Southall

1 January 1901
Armstrong '388' class 0-6-0: 682
'455' class 'Metro' 2-4-0T: 614, 969, 973, 974, 982, 986, 1417
'517' class 0-4-2T: 526, 563, 1470
'850/1901' class 0-6-0T: 1961, 1984, 1990
'1016' class 0-6-0T: 1058, 1060
'1076' class 0-6-0T: 1177, 1288, 1565, 1566, 1568, 1652
'1701/1854' class 0-6-0T: 1759, 1870, 1885
'2301' class 'Dean Goods' 0-6-0: 2338, 2497, 2505, 2511, 2514, 2529
'2361' class 0-6-0: 2370, 2377
'2721' class 0-6-0T: 2724, 2726, 2729, 2739, 2740, 2753, 2756, 2778, 2779

Total: 42

Southall

1 January 1920
455 class 'Metro' 2-4-0T: 1404, 1406, 1420, 3500, 3562, 3565, 3583, 3585, 3590, 3598, 3599
'517' class 0-4-2T: 518, 562, 828, 1161, 1163
'850' class 0-6-0T: 1931.
'1661' class 0-6-0T: 1675, 1681, 1687
'1701/1854' class 0-6-0T: 1730, 1769, 1793, 1872, 1880
'2021' class 0-6-0T: 2083, 2101, 2103
'2201' class 2-4-0: 2220

'2301' class 'Dean Goods' 0-6-0: 2465, 2472, 2474, 2531, 2540
'2721' class 0-6-0T: 2752, 2764
'28xx' class 2-8-0: 2882
'4300' class 2-6-0: 4362, 4381

Southall

1 January 1930
'455' class 'Metro' 2-4-0T: 976, 982, 1404, 1409, 1416, 1453, 3562, 3565, 3566, 3583, 598
'517' class 0-4-2T: 526, 554, 828, 830, 1159, 1160, 1438, 1470, 1484
'645' class 0-6-0PT: 1538
'850' class 0-6-0PT: 1994
'1076' class 0-6-0PT: 1237, 1282, 1659
'1661' class 0-6-0PT: 1696
'1813' class 0-6-0PT: 1848, 1850
'2021' class 0-6-0PT: 2072
'2301' class 'Dean Goods' 0-6-0: 2393, 2489, 2556
'2361' class 0-6-0: 2361, 2374
'28xx' class 2-8-0: 2843, 2844, 2851
'33xx' class 'Bulldog' 4-4-0: 3389
'39xx' class 2-6-2T: 3902, 3919
'43xx' class 2-6-0: 6307, 6382, 6391
'45xx' class 2-6-2T: 4593, 4594, 5500
'57xx' class 0-6-0PT: 5727, 5744

Total: 48

Southall

1 January 1940
'455' class 'Metro' 2-4-0T: 3585, 3596
'2251' class 0-6-0: 2285
'28xx' class 2-8-0: 2845, 2856, 2858
'43xx' class 2-6-0: 9300, 9301, 9304, 9310
'48xx' class 0-4-2T: 4826
'54xx' class 0-6-0PT: 5401, 5405, 5408, 5409, 5410, 5411, 5413, 5414, 5415, 5416, 5417, 5418, 5420, 5421
'57xx' class 0-6-0PT: 3620, 3704, 3750, 3799, 5727, 5737, 5755, 7710, 7730, 7731, 7732, 8752, 8755, 8758, 8764, 8774, 9731, 9755
'61xx' class 2-6-2T: 6110, 6112, 6115, 6118, 6125, 6128, 6139, 6146, 6147, 6148, 6156, 6169

Total: 55

Southall

1 January 1950
'850' class 0-6-0ST: 1925
'16xx' class 0-6-0PT: 1605
'2251' class 0-6-0: 2285
'28xx' class 2-8-0: 2843, 2858, 3803, 3854, 3855, 3856, 3857
'43xx' class 2-6-0: 5356, 5360, 6325, 6388, 9300, 9301, 9310, 9311
'48xx' class 0-4-2T: 1443, 1462
'49xx' Hall class 4-6-0: 4917 *Crosswood Hall*, 4944 *Middleton Hall*, 4978 *Westwood Hall*, 5983 *Henley Hall*, 5989 *Cransley Hall*
'54xx' class 0-6-0PT: 5401, 5405, 5410, 5414, 5415, 5416, 5418, 5420
'57xx' class 0-6-0PT: 3618, 3704, 3727, 3750, 3799, 4608, 4610, 4673, 4695, 5727, 5751, 5753, 5755, 5799, 7730, 7731, 7732, 8752, 8758, 8774, 9641, 9726
'61xx' class 2-6-2T: 6102, 6110, 6125, 6126, 6128, 6139, 6147, 6148, 6156, 6165, 6169
'6959' 'Modified Hall' 4-6-0: 6961 *Stedham Hall*
'94xx' class 0-6-0PT: 9407, 9409
Ex-GW Diesel Railcars: W17, W34

Total: 71

Southall

1 January 1960
'15xx' class 0-6-0PT: 1501
'16xx' class 0-6-0PT: 1669
'47xx' class 2-8-0: 4707
'48xx' class 0-4-2T: 1431

'49xx 'Hall' class 4-6-0: 4907 *Broughton Hall*, 4925 *Eynsham Hall*, 4934 *Hindlip Hall*, 4996 *Eden Hall*, 5918 *Walton Hall*, 5925 *Eastcote Hall*, 5933 *Kingsway Hall*, 5996 *Mytton Hall*
'54xx' class 0-6-0PT: 5410.
'57xx' class 0-6-0PT: 3618, 3620, 3704, 3715, 3750, 3799, 4608, 4673, 8750, 8752, 8761, 8769, 8774, 9641, 9642, 9726, 9739
'61xx' class 2-6-2T: 6110, 6128, 6133, 6144, 6147, 6148, 6149, 6156, 6157, 6159, 6165, 6169
'69xx 'Modified Hall' class 4-6-0: 6967 *Willesley Hall*, 6991 *Acton Burnell Hall*, 7910 *Hown Hall*
'94xx' class 0-6-0PT: 8413, 8451, 8456, 9409, 9413, 9422, 9490
Ex-GW Diesel Railcars: W21, W25, W27, W31, W34
Ex-WD 2-8-0: 90174, 90355, 90356, 90466, 90630
Class 08 Diesel: D3196, D3753, D3754, D3761, D3762
Total 62

Southall

Final Steam Allocation September 1965
'61xx' class 2-6-2T: 6106, 6112, 6117, 6132, 6134, 6135, 6141, 6143, 6156, 6160, 6161
BR Standard Class 9F 2-10-0: 92216, 92240, 92241, 92246
Class 08 Diesel: D3354, D3527, D3754, D3761, D3763, D3772
Total 21

3. Signalboxes

Paddington-Twyford Section	Date Closed	Frame
Paddington Arrival	12 November 1967	141
Paddington Departure	15 October 1967	96
Westbourne Bridge	15 October 1967	88
Subway Junction	19 November 1967	96
Portobello Junction	18 September 1967	91
Ladbroke Grove	18 September 1967	117
Old Oak Common Engine Shed	15 December 1977	38
Old Oak Common East	8 October 1962	160
Old Oak Common West	8 October 1962	144
Old Oak Common Panel box (opened 8 October 1962 extended 4 September 1967)*		
Friars Junction	8 October 1962	71
Acton East	1 February 1959	66
Acton Middle	1 February 1959	52
Acton West (renamed Acton 1/2/59)	24 February 1968	80
Acton West (opened 24/2/68)	5 May 1984	32
Acton Yard (opened 1/2/59)	7 April 1984	58
Ealing Broadway	20 March 1955	65
Longfield Avenue	20 March 1955	24
West Ealing	13 May 1968	71
Hanwell	20 March 1955	45
Southall East Junction	13 May 1968	48
Southall East Station	13 May 1968	123
Southall West Station	13 May 1968	100
Southall West Junction	13 May 1968	55
Hayes and Harlington	10 June 1968	80
Hayes	7 January 1963	24
West Drayton East	9 February 1964	69
West Drayton West	16 May 1960	90
West Drayton West (opened 16/5/60)	21 September 1970	66
Iver	14 October 1963	34
Langley	14 October 1963	41
Dolphin Junction	14 October 1963	47
Slough East	14 October 1963	59
Slough Middle	14 October 1963	101
Slough West	14 October 1963	95
Slough Panel (opened 14/10/63)		
Farnham Road	19 November 1962	74
Burnham (Bucks)	19 November 1962	27
Taplow	20 July 1974	71

	Date Closed	Frame
Maidenhead East	8 December 1963	45
Maidenhead Middle	8 December 1963	59
Maidenhead West	8 December 1963	53
Maidenhead (opened 8/12/63)	21 October 1974	46
Waltham Siding	31 July 1961	43
Shottesbrook	31 July 1961	8
Ruscombe	23 October 1961	38
Twyford East	23 October 1961	31
Twyford West	23 October 1961	61
Twyford (opened 23/10/1961)	20 March 1972	56

*Due to close 1993

New Line:
Old Oak-High Wycombe

North Acton Junction	2 December 1966	32
Park Royal West	15 July 1979	55
Perivale	14 September 1955	13
Greenford East Loop	8 December 1956	23
Greenford South Loop	8 December 1956	23
Greenford Station East		76
Greenford West	8 August 1971	37
Drayton Green	20 March 1955	23
Northolt Junction East	26 May 1990	55
Northolt Junction West	12 July 1966	29
West Ruislip	26 May 1990	45
Denham West Junction	19 December 1965	33
Denham	15 June 1975	41
Gerrards Cross	10 August 1990	33
Beaconsfield	7 December 1975	39
Tylers Green	8 February 1953	6
High Wycombe South	10 August 1990	93

Branch Boxes

Brentford Branch	Date Closed	Frame
Firestone	31 May 1964	33
Brentford Town	31 January 1954	19
Staines Branch	Date Closed	Frame
Colnbrook	12 July 1959	21
Staines West	20 April 1960	14
Uxbridge	Date Closed	Frame
Uxbridge Vine Street	18 October 1962	26
Uxbridge High Street	25 September 1939	14
Windsor Branch	Date Closed	Frame
Bath Road Junc (Slough)	14 October 1963	23
Windsor	5 May 1963	61
Windsor (opened 5/5/63)	17 November 1968	34
Henley on Thames Branch	Date Closed	Frame
Wargrave	3 October 1954	19
Shiplake	14 March 1973	22
Henley on Thames	20 March 1972	54
Maidenhead/Marlow/ Wycombe	Date Closed	Frame
Wooburn Green	4 May 1970	18
Cookham	22 August 1971	18
Marlow	29 September 1954	16
Bourne End South	30 January 1956	55
Bourne End North	22 August 1971	44
Loudwater	4 May 1970	25

West London Line	Date Closed
Viaduct Junction	27 April 1975
Kensington North Main	22 January 1983.
Kensington Middle	23 February 1958
Kensington South Main	4 October 1992
Lillie Bridge Sidings	22 November 1974
Earls Court Junction	23 February 1958
West Brompton	23 September 1956
Chelsea & Fulham	11 September 1981
Battersea	16 March 1936

Frame size (number of levers) given as at closure.

'Britannia' class 4-6-2 No 70026 *Polar Star* leaves Paddington with the 1.55pm service to Pembroke Dock. This was the engine that was involved in the accident at Milton, near Didcot, on 22 November 1955. *Eric Treacy*